Grade 6 English

SPELLING WORKBOOK

Weekly Targeted Practice Worksheets & Spelling Tests

6TH Grade English
Ages 11-12

About This Workbook

Designed to make spelling more engaging for Grade 6 students, this targeted workbook uses a **fresh approach** to help students **improve their spelling skills** over the course of the year.

Combining areas of spelling that 6th graders need to master with a range of topics that they actually find interesting, this workbook contains **36 units — one for every week of the school year (plus 3 BONUS UNITS!)**, each made up of a **worksheet** followed by a **20-sentence spelling test**.

Each worksheet provides students with
- **Targeted lists of 20 words** to be learned
- **Brief descriptions** of the **words** & the **spelling patterns** covered (where appropriate)
- **Bite-size tasks** to encourage them to evaluate their familiarity with, and their usage of, the target words

Additionally, all the worksheets contain a mix of
- **Cheat Codes** that reveal tricks to make learning the target words easier
- **Power Speller's Tips** that take a closer look at relevant spelling rules (plus alternative spellings)
- **Notable Mnemonics & Brilliant Breakdowns** that provide further spelling-learning strategies
- **Vocabulary Builders** which point out connections between the week's target words
- **Synonym Spotters & Antonym Alerts** which draw attention to words with similar and/or opposite meanings within the target list
- **Homophone Hunts & Homonym Hassles** which highlight possible word confusion
- **Word Nerd Facts** which identify word origins & interesting facts about selected target words

At the end of the workbook, parents and teachers will also find
- **Suggestions** on how to **administer and grade the tests**
- **Full transcripts** for all 39 spelling tests
- **Suggested Answers** to prompts in Vocabulary Builders, Synonym Spotters, & Antonym Alerts
- **Indexes** to the spelling rules & patterns and themes covered in the workbook organized by (1) areas and (2) units

How To Use It

As the units are **self-contained**, they can be worked through **in order or** used for **focused practice**. In either case, we recommend that students
- Read the **Tips for Students** included at the start of the workbook
- Focus on **one unit a week**
- Take sufficient time to **absorb the information on the worksheets** and **complete the activities** in stages **BEFORE** attempting to learn the target words and doing the spelling test
- Identify the **spelling-learning strategies** they are **most comfortable with** & use them
- Revisit the worksheets as often as they need to

Kindly note: while **this workbook is a stand-alone volume**, its worksheets and tests **reinforce many of the words included** in our *Spelling Words for 6th Grade: 2,000 Words Every Student Should Know.*

Published by STP Books
An imprint of Swot Tots Publishing Ltd
Kemp House
152-160 City Road
London EC1V 2NX

www.swottotspublishing.com

Text, design, and layout © Swot Tots Publishing Ltd. First published 2021.

Swot Tots Publishing Ltd have asserted their moral right under the Copyright, Designs and Patents Act, 1988, to be identified as the author of this work.

Typeset, cover design, and inside concept design by Swot Tots Publishing Ltd.

British Library Cataloguing-in-Publication Data. A catalogue record for this book is available from the British Library.

ISBN 978-1-912956-43-2

CONTENTS

TIPS FOR STUDENTS   4

UNITS

#1 Double Trouble   5

#2 Friend...Or Foe?   7

#3 Sherlock Holmes & Co.   9

#4 They Asked, We Replied   11

#5 Un- The Unheeded   13

#6 That's Just Plain Silly!   15

#7 The Game is Afoot   17

#8 Happy Endings I   19

#9 Sound Effects   21

#10 The Age of Chivalry?   23

#11 Nessing Things Up   25

#12 Spoiled for Choice I   27

#13 Ill- The Ill-Informed   29

#14 Ancient Origins   31

#15 That Doesn't Look Right...   33

#16 Pirates!!   35

#17 Left, Right, Left, Right...   37

#18 Happy Endings II   39

#19 And the Winner is...   41

#20 Dotting I's & Crossing T's   43

#21 En- The Enriched   45

#22 Light Effects   47

#23 All that Glitters...   49

#24 Well- The Well-Fed   51

#25 Spoiled for Choice II   53

#26 Drip...Drip...Drip   55

#27 Loanwords   57

#28 'Ch' is for 'Chaos'   59

#29 Player 1 is Ready   61

#30 What's it Worth?   63

#31 Happy Endings III   65

#32 How Awful!   67

#33 Bygone Days   69

#34 Out- The Outnumbered   71

#35 The Silver Screen   73

#36 City Central   75

BONUS UNITS

#37 Bookish Business   77

#38 The Big Top   79

#39 That's a Proper Word?!?!   81

NOTES FOR PARENTS & TEACHERS   83

SPELLING TESTS TRANSCRIPTS   84

SUGGESTED ANSWERS   104

INDEXES   106

Tips For Students
Ways To Learn New Spellings

By now, you'll know there are lots of different ways to help you learn new spellings — some of which work better for you than others. But, just as a quick refresher, here are some of the most common ones that you might have already used:

I. Look, Say, Cover, Write, & Check...

This is where you
- Look carefully at a word
- Say it aloud to yourself (including silent letters!)
- Cover the word
- Write it down somewhere, and then
- Check to see if you got it right!

II. Mnemonics...

This is where you come up with a funny sentence based on the letters of the word you're trying to learn. For example, to help yourself remember how to spell the word **dent** (d-e-n-t), you could come up with a sentence like

Don't **e**at **N**oel's **t**urtle!

III. Write Your Own Sentences...

This is where you think of a sentence of your own that contains the word and write it down. (We find funny or imaginative sentences work best for us!)

IV. Pattern Spotting...

This is where you look at a list of words and try to find patterns of letter strings that words have in common. (Basically, it's like playing 'Spot The Differences' with words!)

V. Listen, Spell, & Write...

This is where you get someone (e.g. your parent, teacher, a sibling, or even a friend!) to read the words out to you for you to write down. (Alternatively, you could record yourself reading the words, and then play your recording back to yourself!)

* * * * * *

If some of these techniques are new to you, why don't you give them a go?
You might find that they make learning spellings a bit easier.
It's not a problem if they don't, but there's never any harm in trying.
(Plus, if you discover that there are several different techniques that work for you,
it will make learning spellings more varied!)

GOOD LUCK!

#1 Double Trouble

This Week's Target Words!

accommodate	erroneous
accused	essence
ambassadors	gimmick
apparel	occult
attached	syllabus
attendees	symmetry
bulletins	tattoo
colloquial	territory
currency	utterance
efficacy	warranty

CHEAT CODES!

All of this week's twenty words contain a pair of doubled consonants, but there are **three sneaky words that have TWO PAIRS of doubled letters:**

a**cc**o**mm**odate

a**tt**end**ee**s

ta**ttoo**

To remember these three words, why not come up with a funny/silly sentence that contains them all? Possibly something like:

*To **accommodate** Tina, each of the **attendees** got a **tattoo**.*

Bonus: this will also help you remember that all the other words in your list **only have one pair of doubled letters**.

WORD NERD FACT

We're not sure who came up with the word **gimmick** — so we don't know when they came up with it either!

A. About these words...

The thing that all these words have in common is that they all have **at least one pair of doubled consonants**.

B. Head Count...

Have a look at the questions below. Then, read all of this week's target words carefully. Once you've done that, come back and answer these questions.

How many of these words do you **definitely know**? _____

How many of these words do you **sort of know**? _____

How many of these words **haven't you seen before**? _____

C. The Top 5...

Before you start learning these words, make a note here of the **five** that you think will be the **trickiest** to remember:

_____

_____

_____

_____

_____

Why do you think these will be the most challenging for you to learn?

BRILLIANT BREAKDOWNS

Breaking down long words into smaller units can help you remember them:

accommodate: ac•com•mo•date
efficacy: ef•fi•ca•cy
symmetry: sym•me•try
utterance: ut•ter•an•ce

TEST #1: Feeling confident you've learned this week's words? Then give this test a go!

1. The free, plastic toy that comes with those cereals is just a marketing _____.

2. "Cool" is one of my least favorite _____ terms.

3. In protest at recent events, many _____ have been recalled from that country.

4. Students and teachers alike have complained that the _____ is too long.

5. Dr. Dee's shelves held many books that dealt with the _____.

6. Lucinda gave _____ to what we were all thinking, but couldn't say.

7. For years, this _____ has been a source of tension in the region.

8. The charm of this design lies in its lack of _____.

9. The conference _____ were told to gather in the hotel's lobby.

10. "These results must be _____; they make no sense," the scientist declared.

11. I am extremely _____ to my old jeans; I've traveled everywhere in them.

12. The _____ of this new cure is being debated by the medical profession.

13. Nat wants to get a _____, but his mother keeps refusing to let him.

14. That spacious SUV can _____ up to eight passengers.

15. The drachma used to be the _____ of Greece before the euro was introduced.

16. The _____ of Keyla's argument is that she thinks we're right.

17. Jordan has just _____ me of losing our train tickets.

18. Petronella wondered at the costly _____ of the king's guests.

19. The government is issuing regular _____ to keep us updated.

20. If the device is no longer under _____, I'm afraid I can't fix it.

How well did you do?   Total Score: _____ / 20

#2 Friend...Or Foe?

A. About these words...

The words in this week's list are divided into two word clusters:

Cluster 1 (affable, amicably ... neighborly) contains words related to **friends & friendliness**.

Cluster 2 (adversary, combatants ... tussle) contains words related to **adversaries & hostility**.

B. Head Count...

Have a look at the questions below. Then, read all of this week's target words carefully. Once you've done that, come back and answer these questions.

How many of these words *don't you use*? _____

How many of these words do you *often use*? _____

How many of these words do you *sometimes use*? _____

C. The Top 5...

Before you start learning these words, make a note here of the **five** that you think will be the **easiest** to remember:

_____

_____

_____

_____

_____

Why do you think these will be the most straightforward for you to remember?

This Week's Target Words!

affable	adversary
amicably	combatants
befriended	dogfight
camaraderie	foray
cordial	fray
crony	melee
genial	nemesis
inseparable	saboteurs
jovial	skirmish
neighborly	tussle

D. Notable Mnemonic...

S-A-B-O-T-E-U-R-S

Silly **a**pes **b**ought **o**ver **t**wenty **e**normous **u**nwearable **r**ipped **s**hirts.

Now try coming up with one of your own!

Word: _____

Mnemonic: _____

_____

_____

POWER SPELLER'S TIP

The word **melee** can also be correctly spelled **mêlée**.

WORD NERD FACTS

Nemesis is one of the many words in English that come from Greek.

It's also the **name of the ancient Greek goddess** of retribution (i.e. punishment)!

TEST #2: Find out how well you remember this week's words!

1. Professor Moriarty, Sherlock Holmes's _____, gave a long, low laugh.

2. Lilly and Lola managed to resolve their differences _____.

3. Despite their rivalry, the two teams have a _____ relationship with each other.

4. The _____ among the soldiers was plain for all to see.

5. Jim and his _____, Bob, are planning to gate-crash the party.

6. The courageous knight charged into the thick of the _____.

7. We thanked our hosts for creating such a _____ atmosphere.

8. The young elf was _____ by a group of gnomes.

9. In a _____ between Batman and Spider-Man, who would win?

10. I've never seen Uncle Ewan in such a _____ mood; he can't stop smiling!

11. A small group of soldiers made a lightning _____ into the enemy camp.

12. "How very _____ of you to help me, dear!" said the old lady gratefully.

13. Jack and Jill are _____; they go everywhere together.

14. Several people were hurt in the _____ that broke out near the stadium.

15. The debate between the two candidates descended into an undignified _____.

16. Unnamed _____ are being blamed for the factory explosion.

17. Before the fight began, the _____ sized each other up.

18. Angela is such an _____ person; she's so easy to talk to!

19. Reports are coming in of a _____ along the border.

20. Olivia defeated her old _____, Viola, in the semifinals.

How well did you do?   Total Score: _____ / 20

#3 Sherlock Holmes & Co.

A. About these words...

All the words in this list are related to the **super sleuthing world of detectives —** whether they're real or imaginary.

B. Head Count...

Have a look at the questions below. Then, read all of this week's target words carefully. Once you've done that, come back and answer these questions.

How many of these words do you *sort of know*? _____

How many of these words *haven't you seen before*? _____

How many of these words do you *definitely know*? _____

C. The Top 5...

Before you start learning these words, **imagine you are going to write a detective story.** Decide which **five** of this week's words you would find the **most useful** and write them down here:

_____

_____

_____

_____

Why have you chosen these five words?

This Week's Target Words!

criminal underworld	private investigator
deduction	shadowing
forensics	sleuths
gangsters	surveillance
implications	suspicions
informant	testimony
intelligence	victim
investigative	villainy
mafia	wiretap
mobsters	witnessed

VOCABULARY BUILDER

This list contains several sets of related words:

* **Groups of criminals:** criminal underworld | gangsters | mafia | mobsters
* **Names for detectives:** private investigator | sleuths

Can you come up with any more groups? *(Clue: watching)*

WORD NERD FACT

The word **sleuth** comes from the Norse word *sloth*, which means 'trail'.

D. Notable Mnemonic...

F-O-R-E-N-S-I-C-S

Fiona **o**bserved **R**icky **e**ating **n**asty **s**lugs **i**n **C**lara's **S**UV.

Now try coming up with one of your own!

Word: _____

Mnemonic: _____

_____

TEST #3: Think you've mastered your words for the week? If so, carry on!

1. The current _____ are that the culprit will soon be apprehended.

2. The psychiatrist's _____ greatly influenced the jury's verdict.

3. In *The Sign of Four*, Sherlock Holmes's _____ skills are stretched to the limit.

4. Al Capone is possibly one of the most famous _____ of the twentieth century.

5. Mr. Jacobs hired a _____ to look into his business rival's activities.

6. The moral of the story is that _____ is always punished.

7. Government agents installed a _____ on the suspect's phone.

8. Unfortunately, Ron was a _____ of identity theft last year.

9. The _____ has been rocked by the arrest of its most notorious member.

10. After several weeks of _____ Mrs. Green, I decided she was innocent.

11. Over the years, Hollywood has released innumerable _____ movies.

12. He discovered he had been under police _____ for six months.

13. It does not take much _____ to work out who ate all the pie.

14. The _____ threatened to harm Pierre's family if he did not cooperate.

15. Our _____ that our system was hacked have now been confirmed.

16. TV _____ lead far more exciting lives than their real-life counterparts.

17. The _____ waited nervously under the bridge in the dark.

18. "We've received _____ that will help us crack the case," the captain stated.

19. Mrs. Singh _____ her neighbor's car being vandalized.

20. The recent developments in _____ are mind-boggling.

How well did you do?   Total Score: _____ / 20

#4 They Asked, We Replied

This Week's Target Words!

admitted	interrupted
begged	lectured
beseeched	moaned
bragged	pleaded
commanded	preached
confessed	reiterated
exclaimed	requested
grumbled	responded
instructed	retorted
interrogated	warned

SYNONYM SPOTTING

As you might expect, this list contains several sets of synonyms:

* admitted = confessed
* begged = beseeched
* grumbled = moaned
* instructed = lectured

Can you see any other pairs of synonyms in your list?

BRILLIANT BREAKDOWNS

Breaking down long words into smaller units can help you remember them:

admitted: ad•mit•ted
confessed: con•fes•sed
interrogated: in•ter•ro•gated
reiterated: re•it•er•a•ted

WORD NERD FACT

The word **grumble** comes from the sixteenth-century Dutch word **grommelen**.

A. About these words...

All the words in this week's list are **verbs in the past tense** which are all alternative ways of saying **'said' with an extra bit of meaning**.

TIP: In the future, why not try using them instead of 'said'?

B. Head Count...

Have a look at the questions below. Then, read all of this week's target words carefully. Once you've done that, come back and answer these questions.

How many of these words do you **often use**? _____

How many of these words do you **sometimes use**? _____

How many of these words do you **never use**? _____

C. The Top 5...

Before you start learning these words, make a note here of the **five** that you think will be the **least useful** to you when you are writing a dialogue:

_____

_____

_____

_____

_____

Why have you chosen these five?

POWER SPELLER'S TIP

The one verb in this list that has a doubled consonant that is **not** the result of adding the suffix **-ed** is **confessed** (because the base verb is 'confe_ss_').

TEST #4: See how many words you've got the hang of this week!

1. "I don't actually like scrambled eggs," Melinda _____ to me.

2. "Please, let us stay up to watch the game!" _____ Linus and Lionel.

3. "Don't hurt me!" the cowardly lion _____ the mouse.

4. "Move the siege towers into position," _____ Atticus, the Roman general.

5. "I've just bought the latest iPhone," Francis _____.

6. "Could you bring me some more water?" _____ the customer.

7. "You should never, EVER do that again!" _____ my mother.

8. "My head hurts; I've got a headache," _____ Billy.

9. "I'm telling you that I don't know!" Tim _____ irritably.

10. "But what did you see?!" _____ Davina.

11. "I was the one who broke the vase," Nancy finally _____.

12. "Don't be angry with me," _____ Rachel.

13. "Never go into the woods at night," the old woman _____ the young boy.

14. "I haven't the faintest idea," _____ Candy.

15. "Why do I have to do Jenny's shopping for her?" _____ Ruth.

16. "This project must be completed by the end of the month," _____ the boss.

17. "Where," _____ the FBI agent, "were you last Tuesday at midnight?"

18. "Honesty," Rose _____ primly, "is always the best policy."

19. "I don't believe that for a second," _____ Geoff.

20. "What a wonderful surprise!" _____ Hilda delightedly.

How well did you do?   Total Score: _____ / 20

#5 Un- The Unheeded

A. About these words...

All the words in this week's list are ones that can take the **prefix 'un-'** at their beginnings.

This prefix adds the meaning of either **the lack of** or **the opposite** to the base word.

TIP: Don't forget that the prefix 'un-' has other shades of meaning such as 'not'.

B. Head Count...

Have a look at the questions below. Then, read all of this week's target words carefully. Once you've done that, come back and answer these questions.

How many of these words do you *definitely know*? _____

How many of these words do you *sort of know*? _____

How many of these words *haven't you seen before*? _____

C. The Top 5...

Before you start learning these words, make a note here of the **five** that you find the **most boring**:

_____

_____

_____

_____

_____

Why do you find these five words the least interesting?

This Week's Target Words!

unbiased	unheeded
unbridled	unhinged
uncanny	unnamed
uncharted	unnerve
unchecked	unravel
uncouth	unsavory
unearth	unscathed
unerring	unsuited
unfounded	untapped
unfurled	unwieldy

POWER SPELLER'S TIPS

Five words in this list contain **doubled consonants**:

- **Uncanny & unerring** have doubles because their base words already contain them (ca**nn**y & e**rr**)

- **Unnamed & unnerve** each have a double 'n' because both base words start with 'n' (**n**ame & **n**erve)

- **Untapped** has a double 'p' because its base word (tap) is a single syllable word that ends with 1 vowel + 1 consonant

VOCABULARY BUILDER

We often use the adjective **unbridled** to refer to **unrestrained emotions or speech**.

However, did you know that it can also be used to describe **a horse that is not wearing a bridle**?

WORD NERD FACT

The word **uncouth** comes from the Anglo-Saxon word *uncuth*, meaning 'unfamiliar'.

TEST #5: Feeling certain that you know your weekly words? If so, dive right in!

1. By the end of the tragedy, Lady Macbeth has become completely _____.

2. Yolanda's outfit was utterly _____ to the occasion.

3. My mum has an _____ ability to tell when I'm lying.

4. Thankfully, everyone emerged _____ from the accident.

5. That man bears an _____ resemblance to my grandfather.

6. An _____ informant was the source of the tip-off.

7. "What's in here?" grumbled Pete. "I've never carried such an _____ suitcase before!"

8. The sorceress's warnings went _____ by the stubborn villagers.

9. The government believes there are _____ mineral resources in this remote region.

10. A jury is supposed to remain _____ while hearing the evidence.

11. Our attempts to _____ the mystery of the missing manuscript have failed so far.

12. "How _____ of him to turn his back on you!" exclaimed Aisha to Eva.

13. We watched as the sails of the schooner were gradually _____.

14. Maria wrinkled her nose in disgust at the _____ smells coming from the trash can.

15. As they sailed away, the crew knew they were entering _____ waters.

16. Ross exploded with _____ fury when he heard the news.

17. "We're hoping to _____ valuable artifacts," the archaeologist told the reporter.

18. "If the king's greed remains _____, we shall all suffer," cautioned Merlin.

19. The continued silence began to _____ the audience.

20. The rumors of the company's collapse are entirely _____.

How well did you do?   Total Score: _____ / 20

#6 That's Just Plain Silly!

This Week's Target Words!

absurd	irrational
asinine	irresponsible
balmy	ludicrous
farcical	nonsensical
far-fetched	outrageous
foolhardy	preposterous
frivolous	ridiculous
harebrained	risible
idiotic	senseless
inane	unreasonable

CHEAT CODES!

Although quite a few of the words in the list begin with prefixes, **only ONE word this week needs a hyphen**:

far-fetched

Why not come up with a funny/silly sentence to remember it? Possibly something like:

Harry the horse hatched a **far-fetched** *plan to free the fairy.*

Bonus: This will also stop you from shoving a hyphen into any of this week's other words — even if you're tempted to!

BRILLIANT BREAKDOWN
Break down long words into smaller units:

preposterous: pre•post•er•ous

WORD NERD FACT
Another meaning for the adjective **asinine** is *like, or resembling an ass (i.e. the animal)*.

A. About these words...
All this week's words are **adjectives** that are **synonyms for 'silly' in some sense**.

TIP: In the future, why not try using one of them to say that something is 'silly'?

B. Head Count...
Have a look at the questions below. Then, read all of this week's target words carefully. Once you've done that, come back and answer these questions.

How many of these words do you **never use**? _____

How many of these words do you **often use**? _____

How many of these words do you **sometimes use**? _____

C. The Top 5...
Before you start learning these words, make a note here of the **five** that you think are the **most fun**:

_____

_____

_____

_____

_____

Why have you chosen these five words?

HOMONYM HASSLES
Be careful not to confuse these homonyms!

balmy (foolish or crazy)
balmy (soothing)
balmy (temperate or mild)

TEST #6: Positive that you're now an expert on this week's words? Then wait no longer!

1. "The accusation that I am the murderer is _____!" fumed Lord Godolphin.

2. Bridget could not explain the _____ fear that suddenly hit her.

3. It was very hard indeed not to laugh at their _____ comments.

4. "It is _____ to think that you can defeat the mage," Tayla told the apprentice.

5. "I think his tale is too _____ to be true," commented Ricardo.

6. Juno specializes in _____ suggestions; she is so impractical!

7. "I really want to call her _____, but that would be rude," Tania said.

8. It is _____ for you to expect me to read a thousand-page novel in one day.

9. "What _____ scheme has the mad professor come up with now?" asked Yasmina.

10. The more _____ the suggestion, the more likely it is that people will talk about it.

11. "Offering to help once the damage is done is simply _____," Indira pointed out.

12. The politician's obvious attempts to lie were _____.

13. The plot of that movie was _____; it was completely unbelievable.

14. We were appalled by the _____ destruction of the ancient temple.

15. "You can't fix a broken window with glue; that's just _____," scoffed Vera.

16. "It would be _____ of me not to warn you of the dangers," Sam said gravely.

17. "That is the most _____ idea I've ever heard," said Fred in disgust.

18. "You haven't been listening at all; your comments are totally _____," complained Willa.

19. "Putting salt in coffee," Pip said to me, "is a _____ notion."

20. "Your _____ attitude to the problem is inappropriate," scolded Jan.

How well did you do?   Total Score: _____ / 20

#7 The Game is Afoot

A. About these words...

This week's words are drawn from the **ruthless realm of hunters & hunting**, both in the animal kingdom and the human world.

B. Head Count...

Have a look at the questions below. Then, read all of this week's target words carefully. Once you've done that, come back and answer these questions.

How many of these words **haven't you seen before**? _____

How many of these words do you **definitely know**? _____

How many of these words do you **sort of know**? _____

C. The Top 5...

Before you start learning these words, make a note here of the **five** that you **most expected** to be included in the list:

_____

_____

_____

_____

_____

Why have you chosen these five words?

HOMONYM HASSLE

Don't confuse **quarry** (prey) with **quarry** (a place from which stone is extracted)!

This Week's Target Words!

ambushed	feral
bloodshed	omnivore
butchering	predators
cadavers	prey
carcass	prowled
carnage	quarry
carrion	scavengers
corpse	snares
devour	stalk
exhausted	swooped

CHEAT CODES!

Three of the four words in this list that start with 'ca' have **two 'a's** in them, even though they don't sound like they do:

ca**da**vers

ca**rca**ss

ca**rna**ge

To remember these words, try to come up with a memorable sentence that contains them all. Possibly something like:

*The **carnage** in the field was terrible: the **carcass** of the man-eating tiger was surrounded by its victims' **cadavers**.*

Bonus: this will also help you remember that, of the 'ca' words, the odd one out is **'carrion'** because it **only has one 'a'**.

VOCABULARY BUILDER

There are **three words** here for **dead bodies**:

- **cadaver(s) & corpse(s)** are used to refer to the bodies of dead human beings

- **carcass** is used to refer to the body of a dead animal

TEST #7: Feeling confident you've learned this week's words? Then give this test a go!

1. Having brought down a young impala, the cheetah proceeded to _____ it.

2. _____ by the chase, the zebra sank to the ground.

3. Under cover of darkness, the wolves _____ the village streets.

4. Having identified its next meal, the eagle _____ down to make its kill.

5. Not all _____ are large creatures; they can be as small as the net-casting spider.

6. An _____ is a creature that eats both meat and plants.

7. With infinite care, the tiger began to _____ through the long grass.

8. I find the _____ of wild animals by poachers deeply distressing.

9. The young gazelle was _____ by three lionesses.

10. The _____ of a victim of a shark attack washed up on the beach.

11. Most big cats are solitary creatures and hunt their _____ alone.

12. Disa stopped watching the wildlife documentary; the _____ was too much for her.

13. The hunter carefully set up a series of rabbit _____.

14. There are reports of _____ hogs causing serious damage to crops in Alabama.

15. Local people are hunting a man-eating tiger which has left a string of _____ in its wake.

16. _____ birds are birds that feed on the dead flesh of other birds or animals.

17. Coyotes will _____ on a wide range of things, including insects and snakes.

18. Vultures circled the elephant's _____.

19. Hyenas are some of the animal kingdom's most well-known _____.

20. As the pride of lions moved on, smaller creatures emerged to feast on the _____.

How well did you do? Total Score: _____ / 20

#8 Happy Endings I

This Week's Target Words!

breakage	sabotage
coverage	seepage
drainage	slippage
heritage	spillage
lineage	stoppage
mileage	storage
orphanage	tutelage
patronage	voltage
percentage	wastage
pilgrimage	wreckage

A. About these words...

The words in this week's list are all ones that end with the **suffix '-age'**.

When added to words, this suffix **forms nouns**.

B. Head Count...

Have a look at the questions below. Then, read all of this week's target words carefully. Once you've done that, come back and answer these questions.

How many of these words do you **sometimes use**? _____

How many of these words do you **never use**? _____

How many of these words do you **often use**? _____

D. Notable Mnemonics...

W-R-E-C-K-A-G-E

While **R**ita **e**ats **c**lammy **k**ippers, **A**rchie **g**uzzles **e**spresso.

T-U-T-E-L-A-G-E

Two **u**rbane **t**urkeys **e**njoyed **L**ady **A**dele's **g**arden **e**vent.

Now try coming up with one of your own!

Word: _____

Mnemonic: _____

_____

_____

C. The Top 5...

Before you start learning these words, make a note here of the **five** that you think you will find the **trickiest** to remember:

_____

_____

_____

_____

_____

Why do you think these five will be the most challenging?

POWER SPELLER'S TIPS

Lineage & mileage keep the letter 'e' from their base words (line & mile).

Storage & wastage lose the letter 'e' from their base words (store & waste).

THE ODD ONE OUT

Sabotage is the only word in this list in which **'-age' is pronounced differently**. It should be pronounced **as if it were spelled 'ahj'**.

TEST #8: Find out how well you remember this week's words!

1. The train _____ is being searched for survivors.

2. Catherine can trace her _____ back to the reign of George III.

3. _____ may have caused the plane crash.

4. This antique writing desk is a prized part of our family _____.

5. The hero of the novel I'm reading grew up in an _____.

6. "Could you explain what _____ time is?" Misha asked.

7. If we were all a bit more careful, we could drastically reduce global food _____.

8. The media's _____ of this election has been relentless.

9. A car's _____ is one factor that affects its resale value.

10. The _____ from these old batteries has ruined the remote control.

11. During the Renaissance, _____ was one way for artists to earn money.

12. High-_____ fences have been erected around the chemical plant.

13. Under the philosopher's _____, the young princess acquired much wisdom.

14. The soles of these boots are designed to prevent _____.

15. Avoid unwanted _____ by firmly tightening the cap on the bottle.

16. I've taken out insurance for my phone to cover screen _____.

17. "Do you know what _____ of the population buys newspapers?" Andy asked.

18. Graceland is a popular _____ destination for Elvis Presley fans.

19. "How much _____ space has your new laptop got?" Ben inquired.

20. An efficient _____ system is a key element of public sanitation.

How well did you do?   Total Score: _____ / 20

#9 Sound Effects

A. About these words...

This week's words are all **adjectives** that describe **sounds**. Each adjective in the list has a particular shade of meaning.

TIP: If you're unsure what a word means, look it up in your dictionary!

B. Head Count...

Have a look at the questions below. Then, read all of this week's target words carefully. Once you've done that, come back and answer these questions.

How many of these words do you **sort of know**? _____

How many of these words do you **definitely know**? _____

How many of these words **haven't you seen before**? _____

C. The Top 5...

Before you start learning these words, make a note here of the **five** that you think you will use **most often** in your writing:

_____

_____

_____

_____

_____

Why have you chosen these five words?

WORD NERD FACT

Mellifluous comes from two (!!) Latin words: *mel* (honey) and *fluere* (to flow).

This Week's Target Words!

blaring	plaintive
cacophonous	raucous
caterwauling	resonant
clattering	rhythmic
discordant	ricocheting
droning	sonorous
dulcet	staccato
harmonious	symphonic
mellifluous	tumultuous
monotonous	ululating

ANTONYM ALERT

As you might expect, this list contains several sets of antonyms:

- discordant ≠ harmonious
- droning ≠ sonorous
- cacophonous ≠ symphonic

Can you come up with antonyms of your own for any of the adjectives in your list?

SYNONYM SPOTTING

Predictably too, this list contains synonyms:

- blaring = cacophonous
- dulcet = mellifluous

Can you find any more synonym pairs in this week's list?

POWER SPELLER'S TIPS

Ironically, at least one of these sound words has a **tricky silent letter**:

r**h**ythmic ('h')

And, for some people, so too does the word

ricoche**t**ing ('t')

TEST #9: Think you've mastered your words for the week? If so, carry on!

1. The field was filled with the sound of _____ bees.

2. Surprisingly, the slight elf had a deep, reassuringly _____ voice.

3. A group of _____ women had gathered outside the bride's home.

4. Bruce's _____ "Silence!" stopped us all in our tracks.

5. Rhoda was kept awake by a _____ animal in her backyard.

6. The birds were quite _____ as they squabbled over the crumbs.

7. Two of Tina's favorite _____ dances are the rumba and the mambo.

8. In a round, several voices begin singing at different points, yet remain _____.

9. The diner's kitchen was filled with the sound of _____ dishes.

10. A _____ crash outside the house brought us all running to investigate.

11. The _____ tones of the choir could be heard outside the church.

12. _____ music was coming from our neighbor's outdoor speakers.

13. The _____ echoes in the cave were quite disorienting.

14. Some contemporary classical music can be quite _____.

15. I've always found playing _____ notes a bit of a challenge.

16. Many composers have produced both _____ works and chamber music.

17. A worrying, _____ thudding started coming from the dishwasher.

18. The mother's low, _____ voice lulled her child to sleep.

19. Heavy metal concerts are nothing if not _____.

20. The _____ mewling of the abandoned kittens was heartbreaking.

How well did you do?   Total Score: _____ / 20

#10 The Age of Chivalry?

This Week's Target Words!

broadsword	longbow
catapult	medieval
chivalrous	parchment
chronicles	pennants
feudalism	pillaging
fiefs	plague
guilds	ramparts
heraldry	tapestry
jester	tournament
lance	troubadour

D. Notable Mnemonic...

M-E-D-I-E-V-A-L

Musical **e**lves **d**anced **i**nto **E**liza's **v**ery **a**rtistic **l**ounge.

Now try coming up with one of your own!

VOCABULARY BUILDER

This list contains groups of related words:

- **Weapons**: broadsword | catapult | lance | longbow
- **Medieval professions**: jester | troubadour

Can you find any more groups of related words? *(Clue: writing)*

WORD NERD FACT

Quite a few of this week's words come from French, including

fiefs | pillaging | ramparts

tapestry | tournament | troubadour

A. About these words...

This week's list is made up of a mixture of words that we associate with the **dramatic world of knights, castles, & the Middle Ages!**

B. Head Count...

Have a look at the questions below. Then, read all of this week's target words carefully. Once you've done that, come back and answer these questions.

How many of these words do you **often use**? _____

How many of these words do you **never use**? _____

How many of these words do you **sometimes use**? _____

C. The Top 5...

Before you start learning these words, make a note here of the **five** that you **least expected** to find in the list:

_____

_____

_____

_____

_____

Why are you so surprised by these five words?

POWER SPELLER'S TIP

Two of the words in this list are **'ie' words**:

f**ie**fs | med**ie**val

TEST #10: See how many words you've got the hang of this week!

1. Seeing his enemy approach, Sir Galahad readied his _____.

2. The arrival of a wandering _____ filled the villagers with excitement.

3. In the Middle Ages, _____ was made from the skin of calves, lambs, or goats.

4. Some of the most famous _____ fields were located in northeastern France.

5. The _____ was favored by English archers.

6. Barry has quite an unusual hobby: the study of _____.

7. The Bayeux _____ is currently in a museum in Normandy, France.

8. "The _____ are silent on the fate of King Stefan the Swift," the sorceress noted.

9. "Summon the court _____," ordered the king. "I wish to be entertained."

10. Exhausted by the fight, the rebel finally lowered his _____ and surrendered.

11. The precise dates of the _____ period are often debated by scholars.

12. The traitors' heads were displayed on the castle's _____ as a grim warning.

13. The travelers could see colorful _____ adorning the castle's battlements.

14. One of the most powerful _____ in Gascony, France, was the county of Armagnac.

15. "How common was _____ in the Middle Ages?" the student asked.

16. The Black Death, or the _____, devastated countless populations.

17. In a _____ act, Sir Tristan gave his last hunk of bread to the starving child.

18. The _____ was a weapon often used during sieges in the Middle Ages.

19. Certain aspects of _____ in the Middle Ages resemble modern-day trade unions.

20. '_____' is not a term that was used in the Middle Ages; it was formulated later on.

How well did you do?   Total Score: _____ / 20

#11 Nessing Things Up

A. About these words...

The words in this week's list are all ones that end with the **suffix '-ness'**.

This is another suffix (like '-age') which **forms nouns** when added to words.

B. Head Count...

Have a look at the questions below. Then, read all of this week's target words carefully. Once you've done that, come back and answer these questions.

How many of these words do you *definitely know*? _____

How many of these words *haven't you seen before*? _____

How many of these words do you *sort of know*? _____

C. The Top 5...

Before you start learning these words, make a note here of the **five** that you think will be the **easiest** for you to remember:

_____

_____

_____

_____

_____

Why do you think these five words will be the least challenging?

BRILLIANT BREAKDOWN

Break down long words into smaller units:

indebtedness: in•deb•ted•ness

This Week's Target Words!

adroitness	ineptness
bluntness	keenness
callowness	nothingness
comeliness	quirkiness
deftness	robustness
exactness	scantiness
foreignness	shrewdness
haughtiness	steeliness
haziness	wakefulness
indebtedness	weightiness

CHEAT CODES!

The only **two words** in this list that **end** with the letter string **'nness'** are

foreig**nness** | kee**nness**

To remember these words, why not come up with a distinctive sentence that contains them? Maybe something like:

*The sorceress's **foreignness** was emphasized by the **keenness** of her vision.*

BONUS: this will also help you remember that **none of the other words** in your list end with 'nness'.

POWER SPELLER'S TIP

Seven entries in this list follow the rule of replacing a word's final 'y' with an 'i' when adding a suffix:

comel**y** ⇨ comel**i**ness

haught**y** ⇨ haught**i**ness

haz**y** ⇨ haz**i**ness

quirk**y** ⇨ quirk**i**ness

scant**y** ⇨ scant**i**ness

steel**y** ⇨ steel**i**ness

weight**y** ⇨ weight**i**ness

TEST #11: Feeling certain that you know your weekly words? If so, dive right in!

1. "No," replied Nancy, with unusual _____.

2. The _____ of evidence is hindering the investigation.

3. With swift _____, the tailor mended the gaping hole in the young man's coat.

4. Although this book is rather strange, I've really enjoyed its _____.

5. Princess Flora was famed throughout the land for her _____.

6. "Our _____ to you shall be eternal," the grateful villagers told the elves.

7. A strange _____ surrounded the ship on the horizon.

8. Staring at the chaos, Gina could not believe Ellie's _____ at filing.

9. Notwithstanding the _____ of the spices it contained, the casserole was delicious.

10. He found the _____ of the decision too much to bear alone.

11. Our anxiety resulted in several nights of _____.

12. You could argue that it is Romeo's _____ that causes the tragedy.

13. The _____ of my father's frown stopped me in my tracks.

14. "Sanjeev's _____ will be his downfall," predicted Xavier.

15. After Wanda left, her footsteps gradually faded into _____.

16. The lost children felt their hunger with an indescribable _____.

17. The _____ with which the politician changed the subject was remarkable.

18. Keira loves _____; however, this does have its drawbacks.

19. A think tank has questioned the _____ of the inquiry.

20. You should never underestimate the _____ of successful politicians.

How well did you do?   Total Score: _____ / 20

#12 Spoiled for Choice I

This Week's Target Words!

ajar	grandiose
antiquated	grimy
avaricious	grotesque
bountiful	hoarse
canopied	immersive
cavernous	intrepid
distorted	opaque
excruciating	searing
exorbitant	spartan
feisty	turbulent

VOCABULARY BUILDER

This list contains several groups of related words:

- **Adjectives with positive connotations**: bountiful | feisty | immersive | intrepid
- **Adjectives with negative connotations**: distorted | excruciating | exorbitant | grimy | grotesque

Can you see any more connections between this week's words? *(Clue: describing people)*

BRILLIANT BREAKDOWNS

Breaking down long words into smaller units can help you remember them:

antiquated: an·ti·qu·a·ted
cavernous: ca·ver·no·us
exorbitant: ex·or·bit·ant
grandiose: gran·di·ose

WORD NERD FACT

The word **searing** comes from the Anglo-Saxon word **searian**, meaning 'to dry up'.

A. About these words...

The words this week are a list of mixed, **powerful adjectives** that are useful for describing all sorts of things from caves to people's characteristics!

TIP: If you want even more words like these, look this week's ones up in your thesaurus!

B. Head Count...

Have a look at the questions below. Then, read all of this week's target words carefully. Once you've done that, come back and answer these questions.

How many of these words do you *sometimes use*? _____

How many of these words do you *often use*? _____

How many of these words do you *never use*? _____

C. The Top 5...

Before you start learning these words, make a note here of the **five** that you think will be **least useful** to you in your writing:

_____

_____

_____

_____

_____

Why do you think you won't find these five words handy?

HOMOPHONE HUNT

Be careful not to confuse **hoarse** (having a rough voice) with **horse**!

TEST #12: Positive that you're now an expert on this week's words? Then wait no longer!

1. As the storm grew, the waves became increasingly _____.

2. Thankfully, we have had a _____ harvest this year.

3. You can't use that photo, the image is too _____.

4. The _____ heat of the sun beat down on them relentlessly.

5. "Could you please leave the door _____ on your way out?" Sandy asked.

6. It was impossible to see anything through the shed's _____ windows.

7. In the middle of the forest, they found a delightful _____ clearing.

8. "Your hands are really _____! What have you been up to?" Tim's sister asked him.

9. The makers of this video game have created an impressively _____ environment.

10. The _____ interior of the palace was stunning.

11. "You don't scare me!" the _____ fairy told the ogre.

12. "I'm not paying all that for a purse; that's _____!" snorted Lisa.

13. A set of _____ gargoyles adorned the building's exterior.

14. The narrow tunnel suddenly gave way to a _____ chamber full of treasure.

15. The _____ adventurer decided to explore a remote part of the island.

16. Roy's study is _____ because he can't stand clutter.

17. When I broke my ankle, the pain was _____.

18. After so much cheering during the game, Kim found she had become quite _____.

19. The _____ accountant swindled several of his clients out of their savings.

20. The shed was full of rusty, _____ machinery that was unusable.

How well did you do?   Total Score: _____ / 20

#13 Ill–
The Ill-Informed

A. About these words...

All this week's words are hyphenated compound adjectives starting with **'ill-'**.

Using this formulation adds the sense of **'in a bad or unsuitable way'** to a word.

B. Head Count...

Have a look at the questions below. Then, read all of this week's target words carefully. Once you've done that, come back and answer these questions.

How many of these words **haven't you seen before**? _____

How many of these words do you **sort of know**? _____

How many of these words do you **definitely know**? _____

C. The Top 5...

Before you start learning these words, make a note here of the **five** that are your **most favorite**:

_____

_____

_____

_____

_____

Why are these five words the ones that you like the most?

This Week's Target Words!

ill-advised	ill-gotten
ill-boding	ill-humored
ill-bred	ill-judged
ill-conceived	ill-looking
ill-considered	ill-mannered
ill-disposed	ill-natured
ill-equipped	ill-omened
ill-faring	ill-starred
ill-fated	ill-suited
ill-favored	ill-tempered

CHEAT CODES!

Every word in this list **begins with ill** (which is *really* easy to spell), so, even though these words *look* long, all you have to do is **concentrate on the second halves**.

AND, you don't have to worry about which words are hyphenated and which words aren't because they are **ALL HYPHENATED**.

SYNONYM SPOTTING

Even though all the words in this week's list begin with 'ill-', there are still several pairs of synonyms here:

* ill-humored = ill-tempered
* ill-bred = ill-mannered
* ill-advised = ill-judged

Can you see any other synonym pairs in your list?

HOMOPHONE HUNT

Don't confuse the **bred** in 'ill-bred' with the word **bread**!

While there are lots of interesting compound words like *sweetbread*, *crispbread,* and even *flatbread*, **ill-bread** is <u>not a proper word</u>.

TEST #13: Feeling confident you've learned this week's words? Then give this test a go!

1. The grouchy old woman was well-known for her _____ remarks.

2. The only response I got from George was an _____ grunt.

3. The *Bellerophon*'s _____ voyage began on December 28, 1876.

4. The plan to attack in the dark was _____; the troops couldn't see a thing.

5. A person who doesn't enjoy reading is _____ to the study of literature.

6. The large, _____ ogre muttered angrily to himself as he stomped away.

7. The campers realized they were _____ for such a sudden change in the weather.

8. Having fooled the townsfolk, the goblin gloated over his _____ gains.

9. With his wily ways and _____ looks, the king's new advisor has few allies.

10. As the battle progressed, the general's _____ plan soon unraveled.

11. "Ignore these _____ signs at your peril," cautioned the elfin queen.

12. "I can't stand an _____ child," sniffed Lady Bracknell.

13. The team looked on in despair at the _____ efforts of their captain.

14. "Being so _____ is not going to get you very far," Hassan warned Amira.

15. "You would be _____ to challenge me," warned the witch.

16. Romeo and Juliet are famous for being _____ lovers.

17. Nobody could have foreseen that the venture would be so _____.

18. "Why is everyone so _____ towards my ideas?" whined Jeremy.

19. The king's decision to invade the neighboring country was _____.

20. I didn't have the heart to tell Penny that her beloved puppy was rather _____.

How well did you do?   Total Score: _____ / 20

#14 Ancient Origins

A. About these words...

This week's list is made up of a **mixture** of words that come from **ancient Greek or Latin** — two languages that have given us *loads* of words!

B. Head Count...

Have a look at the questions below. Then, read all of this week's target words carefully. Once you've done that, come back and answer these questions.

How many of these words do you **never use**?

_____

How many of these words do you **often use**?

_____

How many of these words do you **sometimes use**?

_____

C. The Top 5...

Before you start learning these words, make a note here of the **five** that you think will be the **trickiest** to learn:

_____

_____

_____

_____

_____

Why do you think these five words will be the most challenging?

BRILLIANT BREAKDOWN

Break down long words into smaller units:

phenomenon: ph•e•no•me•non

This Week's Target Words!

acupuncture	estuary
affiliation	fabrication
agrarian	hypocrite
anarchy	hypothesis
bovine	longevity
calligraphy	panacea
confidentiality	phenomenon
dire	schizophrenia
emulate	sycophant
epiphany	synthesis

POWER SPELLER'S TIP

Of the eight words in this list that include an 'f' sound, five words contain the pesky **'ph'** letter string that sounds like an 'f':

calligra**ph**y

epi**ph**any

phenomenon

schizo**ph**renia

syco**ph**ant

vs

a**ff**iliation

con**f**identiality

fabrication

VOCABULARY BUILDER

This list contains groups of related words:

- **Science-related words**: hypothesis | phenomenon | synthesis

- **Medicine-related words**: acupuncture | panacea | schizophrenia

Can you come up with any more groups? *(Clue: dishonesty)*

TEST #14: Find out how well you remember this week's words!

1. A _____ is a person whose actions do not match their words.

2. An _____ society is one whose economy is focused primarily on agriculture.

3. The woman denied she had any _____ to the criminal gang.

4. The Chesapeake Bay is the largest _____ in the United States.

5. Once built, this factory will be dedicated to the _____ of smart phones.

6. The adjective '_____' can be used to describe something as 'relating to cattle'.

7. "Disobedience will result in _____ consequences," the wizard warned.

8. The possible _____ of a red sea urchin is remarkable: two hundred years!

9. My brother has recently developed an interest in _____.

10. The charlatan claimed that his potion was a _____ for all illnesses.

11. Kids will often _____ their parents' behavior.

12. The journalist had to sign a _____ agreement before doing the interview.

13. "Eureka!" yelled Byron. "I've just had an _____!"

14. The term '_____' was first used in the early years of the twentieth century.

15. _____ is one of many treatments that derive from ancient Chinese medicine.

16. "This is an interesting _____," said the physicist, "but it will need to be tested."

17. A '_____' is, in colloquial terms, someone who sucks up to another person.

18. After the mayor's unexpected announcement, the meeting descended into _____.

19. Astronomers are completely baffled by this strange _____.

20. Nitric acid is formed from the _____ of ammonia and oxygen.

How well did you do?   Total Score: _____ / 20

#15 That Doesn't Look Right...

This Week's Target Words!

absence	diligent
accompaniments	expertise
achievements	hygiene
acknowledgment	liaison
buoyant	occasionally
communication	occurrence
consensus	opportunity
convenience	perseverance
desperate	questionnaire
detached	sincerely

CHEAT CODE!

Five words in this week's list contain a sneaky **'c' that sounds like an 's'**:

absen**c**e

convenien**c**e

occurren**c**e

perseveran**c**e

sin**c**erely

In each of these cases, the last 's' sound in the word is actually made by 'ce'.

To remember these words, why not come up with a silly sentence that contains them all? Possibly something like:

*I tell you **sincerely** that the **convenience** of my **absence** was an **occurrence** resulting from my **perseverance**.*

WORD NERD FACT

The word **hygiene** comes from the Greek word *hygieia*, meaning 'health'.

A. About these words...

All the words in the list this week are ones that we all **commonly misspell**: those pesky words that you spell correctly the first time around, but which you still look at and think, 'Is that *right*?!'

B. Head Count...

Have a look at the questions below. Then, read all of this week's target words carefully. Once you've done that, come back and answer these questions.

How many of these words do you **sort of know**?   _____

How many of these words do you **definitely know**?   _____

How many of these words **haven't you seen before**?   _____

C. The Top 5...

Before you start learning these words, make a note here of the **five** that you think will be the **easiest** for you to remember:

_____

_____

_____

_____

_____

Why do you think these five words will be the least challenging for you?

POWER SPELLER'S TIP

Three words in the list contain the **'ie' letter string**:

ach**ie**vements | conven**ie**nce | hyg**ie**ne

TEST #15: Think you've mastered your words for the week? If so, carry on!

1. The architectural _____ of the ancient Romans are well-documented.

2. Reading regularly is one way to improve your _____ skills.

3. Kindly fill out this _____ after the webinar has ended.

4. Becky was a _____ student; she always submitted her coursework on time.

5. Despite being fluent in French, Simona _____ lapses into her native Romanian.

6. "Contact my press _____ officer if you have further queries," instructed the CEO.

7. Happy beyond words, Vanessa was certain she'd never felt so _____.

8. There is no rush to answer this email; you may reply at your _____.

9. Aladdin's _____ was finally rewarded when he discovered the vizier's hidden treasure.

10. Rick's _____ was commented on by lots of people.

11. All over the world, the _____ of extreme weather events is increasing.

12. Dr. Jones is regularly consulted for his archaeological _____.

13. We _____ regret that we cannot currently assist you in this matter.

14. Part of good oral _____ is brushing your teeth regularly.

15. Tony raced down the street, _____ to make it to the station on time.

16. The valiant soldier was given a medal in _____ of his outstanding bravery.

17. Carlos has not always been so _____; he used to be very sociable.

18. The _____ among my family is that my cousin doesn't exercise enough.

19. "This remarkable _____ has allowed us to study this species," stated the botanist.

20. One of my favorite _____ to cheese is chutney.

How well did you do?   Total Score: _____ / 20

#16 Pirates!!

A. About these words...

All the words in this list are related to the **swashbuckling world of pirates** — whether real or imaginary. (And, yes, pirates *still* exist in some parts of the world.)

B. Head Count...

Have a look at the questions below. Then, read all of this week's target words carefully. Once you've done that, come back and answer these questions.

How many of these words do you *sometimes use*? _____

How many of these words do you *never use*? _____

How many of these words do you *often use*? _____

C. The Top 5...

Before you start learning these words, **imagine you are going to write a pirate story**. Decide which **five** of this week's words you would find the **most useful** and make a note of them here:

_____

_____

_____

_____

_____

Why have you chosen these five words?

BRILLIANT BREAKDOWN

Break down long words into smaller units:

ignominious: ig•no•min•i•o•us

This Week's Target Words!

boatswain	ignominious
buccaneers	infamous
corsairs	inglorious
cutlass	marauding
cutthroats	musket
double-dealing	mutiny
doubloons	nefarious
galleon	notorious
gangplank	privateer
gibbet	raiding

SEEING DOUBLE

In this list, you have **five words** with **doubled consonants:**

bu**cc**aneers

cutla**ss**

cu**tt**hroats

ga**ll**eon

gi**bb**et

You also have **three words** with **doubled vowels:**

buccan**ee**rs

doubl**oo**ns

privat**ee**r

SYNONYM SPOTTING

If you expected this list to contain sets of synonyms, then you were right!

- buccaneers = corsairs
- ignominious = inglorious
- infamous = notorious

Can you think of any synonyms of your own for other words in your list?

POWER SPELLER'S TIP

Boatswain can also be spelled as **bosun**.

TEST #16: See how many words you've got the hang of this week!

1. The crew of the *Black Skull* suffered an _____ defeat at the hands of the French navy.

2. A reward of fifty gold _____ was offered for Captain Jack's capture.

3. Many pirates died _____ deaths.

4. Once found guilty of piracy, some people ended their lives on a _____.

5. One by one, the passengers made their way down the ship's _____.

6. To the Spanish, Sir Francis Drake was a _____ pirate.

7. _____ pirates plagued the waters of the Mediterranean Sea for many years.

8. Barbary _____ feature in a number of famous novels, including *Robinson Crusoe*.

9. Sir Henry Morgan made a fortune from _____ the Spanish Main.

10. The pirates were a band of cruel _____ who showed their victims no mercy.

11. Calico Jack was a pirate who was _____ for having two female crew members.

12. The pirates' _____ plan included kidnapping the admiral's son.

13. "Aargh! I've dropped my _____!" yelled the pirate.

14. One government's _____ was another government's pirate.

15. "Alright, lads!" cried the _____. "It's time to get to work."

16. Grinning evilly, the pirate slowly removed his sharp _____ from its scabbard.

17. After weeks of being lost, the crew decided they had no choice but to _____.

18. The first mate was furious when he learned of the captain's _____.

19. "We are tormented by _____ who attack our treasure ships," complained the merchant.

20. The captain of the _____ had no idea that the pirates were already aboard.

How well did you do?   Total Score: _____ / 20

#17 Left, Right, Left, Right...

This Week's Target Words!

barge	roving
careered	scrambled
chaperone	shepherded
escort	slink
flounced	totter
herded	traipse
loitering	traversed
meandering	trooped
mosey	ushered
pranced	waddled

VOCABULARY BUILDER

This list contains groups of verbs that are related to each other:

- **Verbs meaning accompanying another person in some way**: chaperone | escort | herded | shepherded | ushered
- **Verbs suggesting movements of creatures**: pranced (horses) | slink (wolves) | waddled (ducks)

Can you think of any more verbs you could add to this week's list?

D. Notable Mnemonic...

C-A-R-E-E-R-E-D

Carrie **a**nd **R**achel **e**ach **e**at **r**ed **e**els **d**aily.

Now try coming up with one of your own!

A. About these words...

The words in this week's list are **verbs (in a mixture of tenses)** which are all **alternative ways of saying 'walk'** with a bit of extra meaning.

TIP: In the future, why not try using one of them instead of saying 'walk'?

B. Head Count...

Have a look at the questions below. Then, read all of this week's target words carefully. Once you've done that, come back and answer these questions.

How many of these words do you **definitely know**? _____

How many of these words do you **sort of know**? _____

How many of these words **haven't you seen before**? _____

C. The Top 5...

Before you start learning these words, make a note here of the **five** that are your **least favorite**:

_____

_____

_____

_____

_____

Why have you chosen these five words?

HOMOPHONE HUNT

Be careful: make sure you don't confuse **herd** (in 'herded') with **heard**!

TEST #17: Feeling certain that you know your weekly words? If so, dive right in!

1. Having established there was no more food to be found, the duck _____ off.

2. After years of _____ the globe, the world-famous naturalist decided to retire.

3. "Might I _____ you to your table?" the waiter asked politely.

4. Having lost control of her bike, Wilma _____ helplessly down the hill.

5. "Come on, kids," said Melissa as she _____ the twins out of the candy store.

6. "I have _____ the world," said the hero, "and I have never seen a unicorn."

7. Farida _____ into the living room and declared she was going out.

8. Once class ended, the students _____ out into the corridor.

9. Unhappy with my decision, Leanne _____ off in a huff.

10. All Harry could do once his lie was discovered was _____ away.

11. With nothing to do, Julian spent the afternoon _____ around his local mall.

12. "I think I'll _____ on down to the bookstore," Nigel announced.

13. When the fire alarm went off, all the employees _____ to evacuate the building.

14. Carlos made his grandparents laugh as he _____ them into the dining room.

15. "Knock before you enter; don't just _____ in!" Tia scolded her younger brother.

16. "I can't walk in these high heels; the best I can do is _____," grumbled Maya.

17. "You don't have to _____ me," said Ida crossly. "I can see myself out."

18. "No _____ outside the store," read the sign.

19. All I seem to do is _____ from one government office to the next.

20. We were _____ to our seats by an anxious-looking young man.

How well did you do?   Total Score: ____ / 20

#18 Happy Endings II

A. About these words...

The words in this week's list are all nouns that end with the **suffix '-al'**. This is another suffix which, when added to words, **can form nouns**.

TIP: Don't forget that '-al' can also be used to form adjectives (e.g. navy + al = naval).

B. Head Count...

Have a look at the questions below. Then, read all of this week's target words carefully. Once you've done that, come back and answer these questions.

How many of these words do you *often use*? _____

How many of these words do you *sometimes use*? _____

How many of these words do you *never use*? _____

C. The Top 5...

Before you start learning these words, make a note here of the **five** that you find the **least interesting**:

_____

_____

_____

_____

_____

Why have you chosen these five words?

WORD NERD FACT

The meaning of **tutorial** as we usually use it now evolved in the twentieth century.

This Week's Target Words!

acquittal	proposal
appraisal	reappraisal
approval	recital
confessional	rehearsal
deferral	reversal
disapproval	revival
dismissal	survival
dispersal	tutorial
disposal	upheaval
portrayal	withdrawal

POWER SPELLER'S TIP

Thirteen words here follow the **rule of losing their final 'e'** when a suffix is added to them:

apprais**e** ⇨ appraisal
approv**e** ⇨ approval
disapprov**e** ⇨ disapproval
dispers**e** ⇨ dispersal
dispos**e** ⇨ disposal
propos**e** ⇨ proposal
reapprais**e** ⇨ reappraisal
recit**e** ⇨ recital
rehears**e** ⇨ rehearsal
revers**e** ⇨ reversal
reviv**e** ⇨ revival
surviv**e** ⇨ survival
upheav**e** ⇨ upheaval

CHEAT CODES!

This list contains **three pairs of words** that are **almost the same**. The slight differences are marked in bold below:

appraisal & **re**appraisal

approval & **dis**approval

revival & **sur**vival

Bonus: Even though **some** of these words contain **prefixes, none are hyphenated!**

TEST #18: Positive that you're now an expert on this week's words? Then wait no longer!

1. Marsha nodded her head in _____ at her sister's choice of pantsuit.

2. This novel offers a striking _____ of life in contemporary Jamaica.

3. I found an excellent online _____ on how to bake bread successfully.

4. The _____ of the man accused of fraud surprised us all.

5. After all the awful things that had happened, they deserved a _____ of fortune.

6. "The _____ of our troops from the region is a priority," said the general.

7. Ravi frowned in _____ at his naughty son.

8. Jeff's _____ that we swim in the freezing lake was met with silence.

9. "The species' _____ is in the balance," warned the documentary maker.

10. "If we don't hurry, we're going to be late for our dress _____," Selma warned.

11. The impoverished Lady Montague wanted an _____ of her jewelry.

12. There is a strong, _____ streak to this celebrity's autobiography.

13. Last week, my mother attended a magnificent piano _____.

14. "I think my _____ is completely unfair," fumed the angry employee.

15. The correct _____ of waste is something we should all take seriously.

16. The _____ of the large, angry crowd took several hours.

17. Maria has a particular distaste for the _____ that goes with redecorating.

18. The _____ of the exams has caused all sorts of complications.

19. Our _____ of the matter hasn't changed our views.

20. The Renaissance saw the _____ of interest in ancient Greek and Roman literature.

How well did you do?   Total Score: _____ / 20

#19 And the Winner is...

This Week's Target Words!

acclaim	grant
accolade	hailed
applause	homage
approbation	honor
bestow	laurel
commended	medals
conferred	plaque
decorated	saluted
decorations	tributes
distinction	trophy

CHEAT CODE!

Several words in this list contain **doubled consonants**. One easy way to remember which ones they are is to think of them as groups:

<u>ALL the words beginning with 'a'</u>

a**cc**laim

a**cc**olade

a**pp**lause

a**pp**robation

<u>ALL the words beginning with 'c'</u>

co**mm**ended

confe**rr**ed

SYNONYM SPOTTING

As you might expect, this list contains several pairs of synonyms:

- acclaim = applause
- conferred = decorated
- hailed = saluted

Can you think of any synonyms of your own for other words in this week's list?

A. About these words...

All the words in this week's list are drawn from the **exhilarating world of awards, great achievements, & success**.

B. Head Count...

Have a look at the questions below. Then, read all of this week's target words carefully. Once you've done that, come back and answer these questions.

How many of these words do you **sort of know**? _____

How many of these words **haven't you seen before**? _____

How many of these words do you **definitely know**? _____

C. The Top 5...

Before you start learning these words, make a note here of the **five** that you **most expected** to find in this list:

_____

_____

_____

_____

_____

Why do you think these words are among the most likely to be included here?

POWER SPELLER'S TIP

The only word that contains a **doubled consonant** that is the result of **adding a suffix** is

conferred ⇨ confer + ed

TEST #19: Feeling confident you've learned this week's words? Then give this test a go!

1. In the UK, _____ are awarded as part of the British 'honors system'.

2. "I would love to have an honorary degree _____ on me," said Harris wistfully.

3. Janice's approval was the highest _____ I could have asked for.

4. Most countries have special awards that they _____ on their outstanding citizens.

5. The king rewarded his loyal subject by giving him a _____ of land.

6. We have been _____ for setting up a local support group for the elderly.

7. "I refuse to pay _____ to the usurper," said the rightful heir.

8. The director's last movie was very popular and received much critical _____.

9. Everything Joel does is designed to win the _____ of his peers.

10. On their return, the soldiers were _____ as heroes by their people.

11. "In _____ of your victory, we shall have a banquet," King Arthur told Sir Lancelot.

12. As the general walked by, all his men _____ him.

13. My grandfather owned a large collection of _____.

14. The victorious team lifted the _____ amidst much celebration.

15. Ivy was amazed to learn that one of her ancestors was a politician of some _____.

16. "_____ to this famous musician are pouring in," announced the newsreader.

17. That blue _____ commemorates the birthplace of Charles Dickens.

18. Ten firefighters will be _____ for preventing the historic library from burning down.

19. The audience's _____ at the end of the performance was deafening.

20. _____ wreaths were awarded to the victors of the ancient Olympic Games.

How well did you do?   Total Score: _____ / 20

#20 Dotting I's & Crossing T's

A. About these words...

This week's list contains a mixture of words that are all connected to **writing and style** in some way.

TIP: If you're unsure what a word means, remember that you can use your dictionary!

B. Head Count...

Have a look at the questions below. Then, read all of this week's target words carefully. Once you've done that, come back and answer these questions.

How many of these words do you **never use**? _____

How many of these words do you **often use**? _____

How many of these words do you **sometimes use**? _____

C. The Top 5...

Before you start learning these words, make a note here of the **five** that you think you will find the **least useful** in your writing:

_____

_____

_____

_____

_____

Why have you chosen these five words?

This Week's Target Words!

annotate	salutation
communicate	scratched
correspond	scrawl
cursive	scribbled
formulate	signature
longhand	squiggles
marginalia	succinct
margins	typing
penmanship	verbalize
rewrite	verbose

VOCABULARY BUILDER

Several groups of words in this list are connected to each other:

- **Letters & letter-writing**: communicate | correspond | rewrite | salutation | signature
- **Handwriting**: cursive | longhand | penmanship | scratched | scrawl | scribbled | signature

Can you think of any more groups? *(Clue: conveying meaning)*

CHEAT CODE!

Two pairs of words are very similar here. Their similarities are marked in bold:

verbalize & **verb**ose

marginalia & **margin**s

D. Notable Mnemonic...

A-N-N-O-T-A-T-E

A **n**otably **n**asty **o**tter **t**old **A**ndy **t**o **e**xercise.

Now try coming up with one of your own!

TEST #20: Find out how well you remember this week's words!

1. It can be difficult to _____ a simple sentence to express a complex idea.

2. Before email, people used to _____ by writing letters to each other.

3. In the Tower of London, you can see where prisoners _____ their names on the walls.

4. The ability to _____ effectively in writing is an important skill to have.

5. "I'm finding it hard to _____ how I feel," admitted Sean.

6. Seeing the time, Olaf hastily _____ a note to his wife before he rushed out.

7. Whenever my aunt sees my handwriting, she lectures me about my _____.

8. Having spent over ten hours _____, Ben developed cramp in his right hand.

9. 'Dear Sir or Madam' used to be a common _____ in formal writing.

10. That edition of the novel has space for students to _____ the text.

11. "Please, try to keep your answers _____," the attorney requested.

12. Mabel's _____ is completely illegible; I don't know how anyone can read it.

13. "Make sure to write your answers within the _____," instructed the teacher.

14. "You call those _____ handwriting?" scoffed Martina.

15. When I was at school, my teachers insisted I learn _____ writing.

16. Polly decided that she needed to _____ her composition before handing it in.

17. Working in _____ is easier than typing, I find.

18. While much fiction is full of beautiful descriptions, some can be rather _____.

19. The detectives spent hours trying to decipher the _____ at the bottom of the note.

20. This copy of the anthology is full of the poet's own _____.

How well did you do? Total Score: _____ / 20

#21 En- The Enriched

This Week's Target Words!

encapsulates

encircled

encoded

encompass

encrypt

endear

enfeebled

engulfed

enliven

enmeshed

enraptured

enshrined

enslaved

ensnared

entangled

enthralled

entombed

entrenched

entwined

envision

CHEAT CODE!

Even if you don't know the meanings of some of these words, the spellings of quite a few of them are easy!

All you have to do is **look at the word after the prefix 'en-'** and then you'll discover that you almost certainly already know the words!

~~en~~**circled**

~~en~~**coded**

~~en~~**compass**

~~en~~**crypt**

~~en~~**dear**

~~en~~**liven**

~~en~~**snared**

~~en~~**tangled**

~~en~~**vision**

BRILLIANT BREAKDOWNS

Breaking down long words into smaller units can help you remember them:

encapsulates: en•caps•u•lates
entombed: en•tom•bed

A. About these words...

All this week's words start with the **prefix 'en-'**.

This prefix can add the sense of **'put into'**, **'cause to be'**, **'provide with'**, or **'cover'** to a word.

B. Head Count...

Have a look at the questions below. Then, read all of this week's target words carefully. Once you've done that, come back and answer these questions.

How many of these words do you **sort of know**? _____

How many of these words do you **definitely know**? _____

How many of these words **haven't you seen before**? _____

C. The Top 5...

Before you start learning these words, make a note here of the **five** that you find the **most interesting**:

_____

_____

_____

_____

_____

Why are these five the most engaging?

SYNONYM SPOTTING

This list contains synonym pairs including:

- ensnared = entangled
- enraptured = enthralled

Can you think of any synonyms of your own for words in this week's list?

TEST #21: Think you've mastered your words for the week? If so, carry on!

1. I _____ that this process will take us three weeks to complete.

2. Ava found herself _____ in a bitter argument between her two best friends.

3. Days of fever had left Mr. Smythe wan and _____.

4. The final section of the *Kryptos* sculpture remains _____.

5. "Being rude will not _____ you to anyone," Juan advised Paolo.

6. They walked along the beach in silence, their fingers _____.

7. This festival promises to _____ a wide range of cultural activities and interests.

8. Despite many theories, we still do not know where Alexander the Great is _____.

9. Overnight, the town was _____ by a massive snowstorm.

10. Tiny diamonds _____ the ring's central sapphire.

11. We were completely _____ by the sculptures we saw at the exhibition.

12. Suddenly, Lavinia realized she was _____ in a plot against the emperor.

13. "These changes shall be _____ in law," the politician promised.

14. Vivian's opinion is firmly _____; there's no way you'll change her mind.

15. Many pieces of software claim to securely _____ your messages, but do they really?

16. "'Blah' pretty much _____ how I feel at the moment," Rita said.

17. King Shahryar was _____ by Scheherazade's nightly tales of adventure and mystery.

18. The more it struggled, the more the fly became _____ in the spider's web.

19. "I think painting my room bright pink will _____ it," Nicky said.

20. After the Romans finally defeated the Gauls, many of them were _____.

How well did you do?   Total Score: ____ / 20

#22 Light Effects

A. About these words...

This week's words are all useful **adjectives** that describe **light and how it can make things look**.

TIP: Try using these words instead of saying something is 'bright' or 'shiny'.

B. Head Count...

Have a look at the questions below. Then, read all of this week's target words carefully. Once you've done that, come back and answer these questions.

How many of these words do you *sometimes use*? _____

How many of these words do you *never use*? _____

How many of these words do you *often use*? _____

C. The Top 5...

Before you start learning these words, make a note here of the **five** that you think will be the **easiest** to learn:

_____

_____

_____

_____

_____

Why have you chosen these five words?

WORD NERD FACT

The word **glaring** comes from the Dutch word *glaren*, meaning 'to gleam'.

This Week's Target Words!

ablaze	glistening
blazing	glittering
blinding	luminescent
burnished	luminous
dappled	lustrous
dazzling	radiant
flaring	shimmering
flickering	shining
glaring	sparkling
glimmering	winking

CHEAT CODE!

The **five words** with **doubled consonants** here can be grouped in little clusters:

dappled & **dazzling**
(both the 'd' words)

glimmering & **shimmering**
(rhyming words)

glimmering & **glittering**
(2 alliterative, rhyming 'gl' words)

ANTONYM ALERT

There are at least two pairs of antonyms in this list:

- blazing ≠ flickering
- glimmering ≠ shining

Can you think of antonyms for any of the other words in your list?

VOCABULARY BUILDER

Predictably, several words in this list are connected to each other:

- **Words used to describe people's eyes**:

glaring | glittering | shining | sparkling

Can you think of any more connections? *(Clue: candles)*

TEST #22: See how many words you've got the hang of this week!

1. As he stepped out, Toby had to close his eyes against the _____ sunlight.

2. The queen's heavy, velvet cloak was shot through with _____ gold thread.

3. The _____ candle cast eerie shadows on the wall.

4. "_____ fires have swept through these forests for days," the news anchor stated.

5. Riding across the plain, the knight's _____ armor made him an easy target.

6. There it lay, _____ on the beach: the largest conch that Simon had ever seen.

7. Kyle blinked against the car's _____ headlights.

8. Harris stopped as he noticed something _____ in the undergrowth.

9. The _____ eyes of the sorceress were an unusual shade of violet.

10. In the moonlight, the _____ surface of the lake looked almost unreal.

11. Everywhere Aladdin turned, there were piles upon piles of _____ treasure.

12. Outside in the courtyard, the pale moonlight _____ the large flagstones.

13. The temple was _____ with the light of a thousand candles.

14. Penelope's attention was drawn to the faint, _____ lights in the distance.

15. Crackling and _____, the bonfire started to grow.

16. Cora screamed when she saw the wolf's _____ eyes.

17. Aida's new watch is all purple apart from the hands which are a _____ green.

18. Mother-of-pearl has a distinctive _____ quality.

19. When they were first built, the pyramids at Giza must have been _____ to behold.

20. The peacock's tail is a _____ explosion of blues, greens, and purples.

How well did you do?   Total Score: _____ / 20

#23 All that Glitters...

This Week's Target Words!

aluminum	pewter
brass	platinum
bronze	plutonium
chromium	potassium
cobalt	silver
copper	sodium
electrum	titanium
magnesium	tungsten
mercury	uranium
nickel	zinc

VOCABULARY BUILDER

There are three notable groups here:

- **Man-made alloys:** brass | bronze | pewter
- **Natural alloy:** electrum
- **Metals used to make alloys:** aluminum | chromium | cobalt | copper | magnesium | nickel | sodium | titanium | tungsten | zinc

Can you think of any other ways to group some words? *(Clue: Greek & Roman mythology)*

WORD NERD FACTS

The word **cobalt** comes from the German word *Kobold*: a name given to a type of unhelpful goblin.

Nickel also comes from a German word: *Küpfernickel*, meaning 'copper devil' because miners used to mistake nickel for copper.

And finally, another name for **mercury** is **quicksilver**.

A. About these words...

This week's list contains a mixture of nouns that are the names of some of the most well-known **metals and alloys**.

B. Head Count...

Have a look at the questions below. Then, read all of this week's target words carefully. Once you've done that, come back and answer these questions.

How many of these words *haven't you seen before*? _____

How many of these words do you *sort of know*? _____

How many of these words do you *definitely know*? _____

C. The Top 5...

Before you start learning these words, make a note here of the **five** that you think will be the **trickiest** to remember:

_____

_____

_____

_____

_____

What makes these five words so challenging to learn?

D. Notable Mnemonic...

C-H-R-O-M-I-U-M

Clara **h**ates **r**aw **o**ysters **m**ost **i**n **u**ncooked **m**eatballs.

Now try coming up with one of your own!

TEST #23: Feeling certain that you know your weekly words? If so, dive right in!

1. One of the uses of _____ is in the manufacture of stainless steel.

2. _____ is biocompatible: it is nontoxic and is not rejected by the body.

3. Owing to its scarcity in the earth's crust, _____ is extremely valuable.

4. The filament in this bulb is made of _____.

5. Around thirteen million tonnes of _____ are produced every year.

6. 'Baking soda' is the common name for '_____ bicarbonate'.

7. An important component of nuclear weapons is _____.

8. Quinoa, spinach, and almonds are all sources of _____.

9. We're having _____ window frames installed in the office.

10. An alternative name for _____ is 'quicksilver'.

11. "I suggest you clean that _____ dish before you polish it," advised Farida.

12. Although it is a metal, _____ is very soft.

13. Since it conducts both heat and electricity, _____ has a wide range of uses.

14. I had no idea that _____ is used to make soap.

15. _____ is a naturally-occurring alloy that was used by several ancient civilizations.

16. Did you know Rodin's _____ sculpture *The Thinker* was initially called *The Poet*?

17. _____ is notable for its resistance to oxidation.

18. Both the ancient Romans and Egyptians used _____ to make decorative items.

19. _____ is used in nuclear power stations to generate electricity.

20. A key component in the production of lithium-ion batteries is _____.

How well did you do?   Total Score: _____ / 20

#24 Well– The Well-Fed

A. About these words...

All this week's words are hyphenated compound adjectives starting with **'well-'**.

Using this formulation adds the sense of **'in a satisfactory or good way'** to a word.

B. Head Count...

Have a look at the questions below. Then, read all of this week's target words carefully. Once you've done that, come back and answer these questions.

How many of these words do you *often use*? _____

How many of these words do you *sometimes use*? _____

How many of these words do you *never use*? _____

C. The Top 5...

Before you start learning these words, make a note here of the **five** that you **least expected** to find in this list:

_____

_____

_____

_____

_____

Why do you find these five words so surprising?

This Week's Target Words!

well-advised	well-groomed
well-affected	well-grounded
well-appointed	well-heeled
well-beloved	well-intentioned
well-conditioned	well-liked
well-connected	well-meaning
well-disposed	well-oiled
well-earned	well-ordered
well-favored	well-placed
well-founded	well-rounded

CHEAT CODES!

Once again, you've got a list of words that are **all hyphenated and start in exactly the same way**.

So, your focus should be on the **trickier second halves of the words**, for example:

well-**affected**

well-**conditioned**

well-**intentioned**

You've also got quite a few words in which the **second halves are words that you probably already know**:

well-**advised**

well-**earned**

well-**liked**

TIP: Why not try dividing the words into two groups: tricky endings & easy endings?

VOCABULARY BUILDER

This list contains several connected words:

- **Attitudes towards people or things**:
  well-affected | well-disposed | well-intentioned | well-meaning

Can you come up with any more links? *(Clue: appearance)*

TEST #24: Positive that you're now an expert on this week's words? Then wait no longer!

1. Feeling _____ towards her brother, Alicia lent him her skateboard.

2. Although _____, Tom's words only aggravated the situation.

3. Being _____, Julia knows many influential people in her industry.

4. "I know your efforts are _____, but I need to do this myself," said Justin.

5. Heads turned as the _____ couple entered the ballroom.

6. "Every other male character in that novel is described as '_____'," grumbled Pierre.

7. Since restructuring last year, the company has run like a _____ machine.

8. The scout was impressed by the high number of _____ players on the field.

9. With its _____ suites and rooms, our local hotel has become a tourist magnet.

10. "You've got to be ridiculously _____ to shop at that boutique!" exclaimed Fred.

11. I was not happy to discover my suspicions had been _____.

12. "Your _____ supporters will be key in this race," noted the campaign manager.

13. I think our team is _____ to win this year's tournament.

14. "We aim to help young people grow into _____ individuals," declared the principal.

15. The eccentric billionaire left the entirety of his estate to his _____ dog.

16. Coach Martin is _____ by his students and fellow faculty members.

17. Lady Bracknell's _____ household was the envy of her friends and acquaintances.

18. After a hectic year, Bernie treated himself to a _____ break in Miami.

19. "You would be _____ to address these issues now," Fran's accountant urged her.

20. Being _____ in research methodologies has been invaluable to me.

How well did you do?   Total Score: _____ / 20

#25 Spoiled for Choice II

This Week's Target Words!

agreeably	lamentably
begrudgingly	lithely
covertly	obnoxiously
diligently	paradoxically
elusively	reproachfully
fervently	sedately
feverishly	spontaneously
frenetically	staunchly
haphazardly	tactfully
incessantly	unpredictably

POWER SPELLER'S TIPS

Only **one adverb** in this list is **NOT formed by adding '-ly'** to the end of a word:

frenetically

This adverb is formed by adding '-ally' to the adjective 'frenetic':

frenetically ⇨ frenetic + ally

Notes:
- While 'frenetical' *is* a word, it is archaic and you may not find it in some dictionaries
- Paradoxically ⇨ paradoxical + ly

SYNONYM SPOTTING

This list contains at least one synonym pair:

feverishly = frenetically

Can you think of any synonyms of your own for adverbs in this list?

ANTONYM ALERT

This list contains at least one antonym pair:

obnoxiously ≠ tactfully

Can you think of any antonyms of your own for adverbs in this list?

A. About these words...

The words this week are a list of mixed, **powerful adverbs** that are useful for describing how all sorts of things are done!

TIP: If you want even more words like these, look this week's ones up in your thesaurus!

B. Head Count...

Have a look at the questions below. Then, read all of this week's target words carefully. Once you've done that, come back and answer these questions.

How many of these words do you **definitely know**? _____

How many of these words do you **sort of know**? _____

How many of these words **haven't you seen before**? _____

C. The Top 5...

Before you start learning these words, make a note here of the **five** you think you will find the **most useful** in your writing:

_____

_____

_____

_____

_____

Why have you chosen these five words?

BRILLIANT BREAKDOWNS

Break down long words into smaller units:

incessantly: in•ces•sant•ly
spontaneously: sp•on•tan•e•ous•ly

TEST #25: Feeling confident you've learned this week's words? Then give this test a go!

1. Aki was _____ surprised when she saw how much was in her checking account.

2. Dervla has always had a tendency to behave _____.

3. My neighbor is great, but he does have a habit of talking _____.

4. _____, his life was saved because he was ill.

5. While his sister wasn't looking, Oscar _____ hid her birthday present in his closet.

6. I spent ten minutes _____ hunting in my purse for the house keys.

7. The dignitaries _____ took their places around the table.

8. As the music got faster, the dancers moved ever more _____.

9. The moment the bell rang, Gloria sprang _____ to her feet.

10. Luna _____ tipped the contents of the tote bag onto her bed.

11. "I'm afraid I can't answer that," replied Jed _____.

12. We have been working _____ all week to get our assignments finished.

13. The twins were _____ opposed to Amani's suggestion.

14. "There's no need for you to be mean to me," said Quentin _____.

15. "Have you considered the fact that he might be right?" she asked _____.

16. Under certain conditions, hay can _____ combust.

17. Lucas has _____ accepted that he needs to apologize to Marcia.

18. _____, we are unable to help you at this time.

19. "Well, if you don't know, why should I?" Eric asked _____.

20. "I _____ wish that this had never happened," said Zenobia sincerely.

How well did you do? Total Score: _____ / 20

#26 Drip...Drip...Drip

A. About these words...

This week's list is a selection of **verbs, adjectives, and nouns** that we use when we are talking about **water**.

TIP: You can also use some of these words to talk about other liquids — but do check first!

B. Head Count...

Have a look at the questions below. Then, read all of this week's target words carefully. Once you've done that, come back and answer these questions.

How many of these words do you **sometimes use**? _____

How many of these words do you **never use**? _____

How many of these words do you **often use**? _____

C. The Top 5...

Before you start learning these words, make a note here of the **five** that are your **most favorite**:

_____

_____

_____

_____

_____

Why do you like these five words so much?

This Week's Target Words!

cascaded	irrigated
condensed	overflowing
drenched	precipitation
dribble	saturated
drizzles	soak
evaporated	spouting
flush	spurt
gushed	submerged
immerse	swamped
inundation	trickle

SYNONYM SPOTTING

Predictably, this list contains synonym pairs:

- dribble = trickle
- saturated = swamped

Can you think of any synonyms of your own for words in this list?

ANTONYM ALERT

The list also contains at least one antonym pair:

- condensed ≠ evaporated

Can you think of any antonyms of your own for words in this list?

WORD NERD FACT

The word **drench** comes from the Anglo-Saxon word **drencan**, meaning 'to cause to drink'.

D. Notable Mnemonic...

I-N-U-N-D-A-T-I-O-N

In **N**oel's **u**nused **n**otebook, **D**ylan **a**ttached **t**errific **i**mages **o**f **n**oodles.

Now try coming up with one of your own!

TEST #26: Find out how well you remember this week's words!

1. He noticed that droplets of water had _____ on the windowpane.

2. We stared in horror as the water _____ out of the widening cracks in the dam.

3. Owing to the amount of recent rain, the ground is completely _____.

4. The flowers had died because all the water in their vase had _____.

5. Sheila noticed a thin _____ of blood just below her left knee.

6. "Ugh! I hate it when it _____!" complained Betty.

7. Make sure that you completely _____ the fabric in the dye.

8. If the rain doesn't stop soon, rivers are going to start _____.

9. "Did you remember to _____?" the young boy's mother asked him.

10. The noise the water made as it _____ over the rocks was deafening.

11. "I'd _____ that shirt before putting it in the washing machine," advised Cleo.

12. "It is crucial that these fields are _____ properly," the farmer told us.

13. Once the river burst its banks, it took just an hour for the entire village to be _____.

14. At around ten o'clock in the morning, lava began to _____ out of the volcano.

15. Tarek wiped a _____ of milk from the corner of his baby son's mouth.

16. When they arrived, the engineers could clearly see the well was still _____ oil.

17. _____ is measured using a rain gauge.

18. Last week, I got _____ in a thunderstorm that came out of nowhere.

19. This _____ shipwreck has been a magnet for treasure hunters for years.

20. For centuries in Egypt, the _____ of the Nile was an annual event.

How well did you do? **Total Score: _____ / 20**

#27 Loanwords

A. About these words...

The words for this week are all ones that we've **borrowed straight from other languages** (which is why they are called 'loanwords')!

TIP: If any of these are unfamiliar, look them up in your dictionary!

B. Head Count...

Have a look at the questions below. Then, read all of this week's target words carefully. Once you've done that, come back and answer these questions.

How many of these words do you *sort of know*? _____

How many of these words do you *definitely know*? _____

How many of these words *haven't you seen before*? _____

C. The Top 5...

Before you start learning these words, make a note here of the **five** that you think will be the **trickiest** to learn:

_____

_____

_____

_____

Why do you think these five words will be the most challenging to remember?

This Week's Target Words!

al dente	in absentia
beaux arts	in loco parentis
carte blanche	in situ
compos mentis	laissez-faire
cordon sanitaire	mea culpa
déjà vu	memento mori
double entendre	per se
enfant terrible	persona non grata
fait accompli	sotto voce
haute cuisine	terra firma

THE ODD ONES OUT

Almost all these loanwords are made up of **two words**. The **three odd ones** out are

in loco parentis
(three separate words)

persona non grata
(three separate words)

laissez-faire
(the only hyphenated loanword)

VOCABULARY BUILDER

This list contains groups of related words:

- **Food**: al dente | haute cuisine
- **The Arts**: beaux arts| enfant terrible

Can you see any more groupings? *(Clue: troublesome people)*

CHEAT CODE!

Even though all these words come from other languages, there is **only one word with diacritics** that you have to remember:

déjà vu

TIP: a diacritic is a mark or sign above a letter that tells the reader that the letter is to be pronounced in a particular way.

TEST #27: Think you've mastered your words for the week? If so, carry on!

1. Kimberly's feeling of _____ unsettled her; she knew she'd not been there before.

2. "The _____ in the song's title is fun — even if it is a bit naughty," confessed Gina.

3. After our turbulent flight, we were relieved to be back on _____.

4. He's given me _____ to make any changes to the design I want.

5. "_____!" cried the fairy. "This is all my fault! Please, forgive me!"

6. "Can you see anything?" whispered Alan _____.

7. "Certain dangerous ideas MUST be contained by a _____," argued the activist.

8. During the Renaissance, a person might keep a human skull as a _____.

9. "We must remain _____ as we carry out our security check," said the flight attendant.

10. Ricky loves French _____; I prefer less complicated food.

11. '_____' can refer to a young person who adopts an unorthodox approach to things.

12. They are renovating that building to preserve its _____ features.

13. Since my parents are away, my Uncle Jove is acting _____.

14. Nick prefers his spaghetti _____: with a bit of bite to it.

15. The statement is not wrong _____, but it is vague.

16. Being a night owl, Iris is never _____ before 10 o'clock.

17. As Sir Thomas Overbury had fled to France, the English court tried him _____.

18. "Do whatever you want!" said Harry with an airy _____ attitude.

19. Given her terrible behavior at my last party, Beatrice is now _____.

20. "I'm afraid it's a _____; nothing can be changed now," apologized Fran.

How well did you do?   Total Score: _____ / 20

#28 'Ch' is for 'Chaos'

This Week's Target Words!

alchemy	chorus
anchored	chronic
archaic	hierarchy
archives	ocher
chasm	orchids
chemotherapy	psyche
chimera	scheme
cholera	scholarly
chords	technology
chorister	trachea

VOCABULARY BUILDER

This list contains several groups of connected words:

- **Medicine**: chemotherapy | cholera | chronic | trachea
- **Greek mythology**: chimera | psyche
- **Knowledge**: archaic | archives | scholarly | technology

Can you come up with any more groups? *(Clue: music)*

HOMOPHONE HUNT

Make sure you don't confuse **chords** (groups of notes played together) with **cords** (ropes)!

WORD NERD FACT

The word **alchemy** comes from the Arabic words *al* meaning 'the' and *kimiya*, which itself comes from the Greek word *kemeia*, meaning 'change' or 'transformation'.

So this word comes from **two words AND two languages**!

A. About these words...

This week's list is made up of a set of tricky words in which the **letter string 'ch' is pronounced 'k'**.

B. Head Count...

Have a look at the questions below. Then, read all of this week's target words carefully. Once you've done that, come back and answer these questions.

How many of these words do you *sometimes use*? _____

How many of these words do you *often use*? _____

How many of these words do you *never use*? _____

C. The Top 5...

Before you start learning these words, make a note here of the **five** that you think will be the **easiest** for you to remember:

_____

_____

_____

_____

_____

Why do you think these five words will be the least challenging to learn?

BRILLIANT BREAKDOWNS

Breaking down long words into smaller units can help you remember them:

cholera: ch•o•le•ra
hierarchy: hi•er•ar•ch•y
trachea: tra•ch•e•a

TEST #28: See how many words you've got the hang of this week!

1. The small ship rocked gently on the waves as it lay _____ outside the port.

2. Sylvia is a complete _____ buff; it's all she can talk about.

3. Patty came up with a crazy _____ to discover who stole her bicycle.

4. During the nineteenth century, _____ swept across the globe.

5. The _____ is a mythical monster with a lion's head, a goat's body, and a serpent's tail.

6. Dean spent hours digging through the local _____ in search of a clue.

7. _____ are my least favorite flowers.

8. Many scientists — including Sir Isaac Newton — have been intrigued by _____.

9. In humans, the _____ is found immediately in front of the esophagus.

10. The earliest known usage of the word '_____' is 1910.

11. "Of course, we didn't tell her!" came the _____ of denials from his friends.

12. The human _____ has long been a subject of serious study.

13. Artists' use of red _____ stretches back to prehistoric times.

14. "With such a beautiful voice, have you considered becoming a _____?" Ida asked.

15. Within the _____ of the British aristocracy, a duke ranks the highest.

16. Many _____ books have been written about Shakespeare's life.

17. "I love the opening _____ of that song!" enthused Wendy.

18. '_____' is used to describe words that used to be common, but which are now rare.

19. Reaching the end of the tunnel, the explorer found a great _____ before him.

20. Poor Amelia suffers from _____ indigestion; she always has a stomachache.

How well did you do? Total Score: _____ / 20

#29 Player 1 is Ready

A. About these words...

All the words in this week's list are related to the **ever-expanding world of video games and gaming**.

B. Head Count...

Have a look at the questions below. Then, read all of this week's target words carefully. Once you've done that, come back and answer these questions.

How many of these words **haven't you seen before**? _____

How many of these words do you **sort of know**? _____

How many of these words do you **definitely know**? _____

C. The Top 5...

Before you start learning these words, make a note of the **five** that you find the **most surprising** to see here:

_____

_____

_____

_____

_____

Why have you chosen these five words?

WORD NERD FACT

We get the word **avatar** from two Sanskrit words: *ava*, meaning 'down' and *tarati*, meaning 'he passes over'.

This Week's Target Words!

artificial intelligence	handheld
avatar	interface
cheat code	multiplayer
console	platforms
controller	quests
demos	role-playing game
downloadable	shoot-'em-ups
game engine	single-player
game pad	split screen
graphics	virtual reality

CHEAT CODE!

Only **three entries here need hyphens** and they happen to be **listed consecutively in alphabetical order**:

role-playing game

shoot-'em-ups

single-player

VOCABULARY BUILDER

Three entries in the list can also be referred to by their **initialisms**:

artificial **i**ntelligence ⇨ **AI**

role-**p**laying **g**ame ⇨ **RPG**

virtual **r**eality ⇨ **VR**

TIP: an initialism is **a kind of abbreviation** that uses the first letter of each word in a compound noun or phrase.

D. Notable Mnemonic...

C-O-N-S-O-L-E

Can **o**ne **n**ewt **s**olve **o**bscure **l**inear **e**quations?

Now try coming up with one of your own!

TEST #29: Feeling certain that you know your weekly words? If so, dive right in!

1. Rania spent the whole afternoon watching game _____.

2. The _____ has replaced things like joysticks, paddles, and keypads.

3. "You can get additional _____ costumes for your character," Kim told Sally.

4. "I've completed over a hundred _____ in that game," Lucy announced proudly.

5. "I've tried the _____ option in that game, but I think it's boring," commented Yara.

6. "Have you used this _____? It unlocks a secret level!" said Chen excitedly.

7. That game is available on all the major _____.

8. Shona was unimpressed by the game's _____; they looked dated.

9. "This game's _____ is confusing; I can't see how to do anything," complained Greg.

10. "Which _____ did you select?" Jamila asked Omar. "I chose the goblin king."

11. This racing game has been updated to support _____ mode.

12. My brothers have always been really good at _____; I'm terrible at them.

13. When I first tried a _____ headset, I became a bit nauseous.

14. This new _____ offers highly immersive fantasy worlds for players to explore.

15. "I prefer _____ games so that I can compete against my friends," said Ed.

16. Michel's parents promised to buy him a new game _____ for his birthday.

17. "Something is wrong with the _____; the buttons keep sticking," observed Ravi.

18. A hundred years ago, _____ was pure science fiction.

19. _____ devices have revolutionized our lives in innumerable ways.

20. There's a bug in the _____; you can't get beyond level thirty.

How well did you do?   Total Score: _____ / 20

#30 What's it Worth?

This Week's Target Words!

cherished	contemptible
esteemed	debased
exquisite	good-for-nothing
inestimable	inconsequential
irreplaceable	paltry
laudable	petty
profitable	tawdry
substantial	trifling
treasured	trivial
valuable	valueless

SYNONYM & ANTONYM SOUP

WARNING! You need to be careful with these words. You **cannot assume** that you can use any of them interchangeably as synonyms or antonyms.

Nevertheless, there are a **few pairs of synonyms & antonyms** in this list:

- cherished = treasured
- petty = trivial
- substantial ≠ paltry
- valuable ≠ valueless

CHEAT CODES!

All **five positive words** that finish with the *ble* sound end with '**-able**':

inestim**able**

irreplace**able**

laud**able**

profit**able**

valu**able**

The **one negative word** that finishes with the *ble* sound ends with '**-ible**':

contempt**ible**

A. About these words...

The words in this week's list form two clusters:

Cluster 1 is made up of **synonyms for valued** (cherished, esteemed ... valuable).

Cluster 2 is made up of **synonyms for worthless** (contemptible, debased ... valueless).

B. Head Count...

Have a look at the questions below. Then, read all of this week's target words carefully. Once you've done that, come back and answer these questions.

How many of these words do you *never use*? _____

How many of these words do you *sometimes use*? _____

How many of these words do you *often use*? _____

C. The Top 5...

Before you start learning these words, make a note here of the **five** that you find the **most boring**:

_____

_____

_____

_____

_____

Why do you find these five words the least interesting?

WORD NERD FACT

Paltry comes from the German word *paltrig*, meaning 'ragged'.

TEST #30: Positive that you're now an expert on this week's words? Then wait no longer!

1. My grandmother gave me an _____ Victorian brooch for my eighteenth birthday.

2. When a currency is _____, this means its value is lowered.

3. Mrs. Fischer ran a highly _____ business selling personalized coffee mugs.

4. "Please, be careful with that statuette!" begged Tina. "It is _____!"

5. "A million dollars is no _____ sum," Michaela observed.

6. "I'm not getting into this _____ debate; I've got better things to do," said Pat.

7. "I'm afraid that this painting is a fake; it is _____," the auctioneer told me.

8. His _____ efforts to help his local community were recognized by the mayor.

9. I think this election will be _____; I don't believe it will change anything.

10. Insultingly, the merchant offered the lad a _____ sum as a reward.

11. His grandfather's diary is one of his most _____ possessions.

12. The governor should be dealing with the big issues, not _____ matters.

13. "It gives me great pleasure to introduce our _____ guest," announced Mr. Franklin.

14. I have always _____ the small medallion that my uncle gave me.

15. The worth of this manuscript is _____; it is one of a kind.

16. That day, the young shepherd learned a _____ lesson in humility.

17. "What a lazy, _____ boy you are!" Tom's aunt scolded.

18. His behavior at the meeting was utterly _____.

19. Cheap jewelry doesn't have to be _____; there are ways to make it look good.

20. "Your efforts have made a _____ contribution to the company," my boss said.

How well did you do?   Total Score: _____ / 20

#31 Happy Endings III

A. About these words...

The words in this week's list are all verbs (in a mixture of tenses) that include the **suffix '-en'**.

Using this suffix adds the senses of either **'cause or come to be'** OR **'cause or come to have'** to a word.

B. Head Count...

Have a look at the questions below. Then, read all of this week's target words carefully. Once you've done that, come back and answer these questions.

How many of these words do you *definitely know*? _____

How many of these words *haven't you seen before*? _____

How many of these words do you *sort of know*? _____

C. The Top 5...

Before you start learning these words, make a note here of the **five** that you think will be **least useful** to you in your writing:

_____

_____

_____

_____

_____

Why do you think these five words won't be that relevant?

This Week's Target Words!

chastened	maddened
coarsen	moistened
deaden	overburden
disheartened	reawaken
emboldened	slacken
hastened	smoothens
hearken	straighten
heighten	strengthen
laden	unburden
lessen	unfasten

HOMOPHONE HUNT

Don't confuse the verb **lessen** with the noun **lesson**!

CHEAT CODE!

This list contains **two pairs of words that are very close in spelling**. The slight differences between them are highlighted in bold:

chastened & hastened

overburden & **un**burden

ANTONYM ALERT

This list contains several sets of antonyms:

• laden ≠ unburden
• disheartened ≠ emboldened
• heighten ≠ lessen

Can you think of any antonyms of your own for verbs in this list?

PRONUNCIATION PUZZLE

The verb **hearken** is tricky to pronounce because it *looks like* it should sound like you are saying: 'hear' + 'ken'.

However, that's not right. The 'hear' in *hearken* should sound like the 'har' in *hard*.

TEST #31: Feeling confident you've learned this week's words? Then give this test a go!

1. The poor horses found themselves _____ with heavy saddlebags.

2. Vitamin D is meant to help _____ bones and teeth.

3. We need to find a way to _____ the negative impact of this.

4. The king's counselors _____ to inform him of the dragons' arrival.

5. "If you need to _____ yourself, you can always talk to me," Lyra told Alice supportively.

6. Chris was utterly _____ by Ro's selfish behavior.

7. Billy was _____ when he realized he had misjudged his brother.

8. Olivia loves her curly hair, so she never tries to _____ it.

9. "Come on! Don't be _____! It's not over yet!" Harriet urged.

10. We are always looking for ways to _____ students' enjoyment of learning.

11. "Can I have something to help _____ the pain?" Brian asked his dentist.

12. According to legend, King Arthur will _____ when Britain needs him again.

13. The makers of this hand cream claim it _____ your skin in a week.

14. "I didn't tell you this before as I didn't want to _____ you," Marina explained.

15. The suspect _____ his lips nervously before answering the question.

16. "_____ to my advice, or calamity will befall the kingdom," the old crone cautioned.

17. The fairy's smile _____ the shepherd to approach her.

18. "Can you _____ these cuff links for me?" Mr. Romano asked his wife.

19. Doing a lot of manual work is likely to _____ your hands.

20. "Now is not the time to _____! We must keep forging ahead!" cried the general.

How well did you do?   Total Score: _____ / 20

#32 How Awful!

This Week's Target Words!

abhorrent	gruesome
abominable	heinous
appalling	horrendous
atrocious	loathsome
despicable	nauseating
detestable	noxious
distasteful	objectionable
distressing	odious
ghastly	repugnant
gross	unwholesome

POWER SPELLER'S TIP

In American English, the **h** in the word **ab<u>h</u>orrent** is pronounced, while in British English, it is not.

However the word is pronounced though, it **must always be spelled with the <u>h</u>.**

CHEAT CODE!

All four words that finish with the *ble* sound end with the letter string '-**able**':

abomin**able**

despic**able**

detest**able**

objection**able**

HOMONYM HASSLE

As it can be used as an adjective, a noun, or a verb, the word **gross** has **lots of different meanings**.

In this list, it's being used in its **informal / colloquial sense of 'disgusting'**.

A. About these words...

The words in this week's list are all **adjectives** which are **slightly different ways of saying 'awful'**.

TIP: The next time you want to say something is 'awful', why not try using one of these words instead?

B. Head Count...

Have a look at the questions below. Then, read all of this week's target words carefully. Once you've done that, come back and answer these questions.

How many of these words do you **often use**? _____

How many of these words do you **never use**? _____

How many of these words do you **sometimes use**? _____

C. The Top 5...

Before you start learning these words, make a note here of the **five** that you find the **most fun**:

_____

_____

_____

_____

_____

Why do you think these are the five words that you enjoy the most?

BRILLIANT BREAKDOWNS

Breaking down long words into smaller units can help you remember them:

abominable: a•bo•min•able
repugnant: re•pug•n•ant

TEST #32: Find out how well you remember this week's words!

1. Although the images were _____, we could not tear our eyes away from them.

2. For the Elizabethans, regicide was a most _____ crime.

3. "Your _____ actions leave me with no choice," the judge told the defendant sternly.

4. The family were devastated by the _____ news.

5. "I can't abide Mr. Collins," said Lydia. "I've never met a more _____ man."

6. "I love my sister dearly, but her taste in clothes is _____," confessed Janice.

7. "I always enjoy a story with a _____ villain," declared Armand.

8. The duke's betrayal of his younger brother was utterly _____.

9. Excessive competitiveness in an office can lead to an _____ workplace.

10. It is not yet known how many people were injured in the _____ accident.

11. The king's chief advisor was a _____ man; he had no scruples to speak of.

12. "I find any kind of deceit _____," said Rosa primly.

13. As the samurai warriors entered the temple, a _____ sight met their eyes.

14. The _____ crimes committed by the gang have shocked the whole state.

15. That magazine always prints _____ photos of celebrities.

16. "The weather has been _____ recently; it's rained constantly," Ivy told me.

17. The smell of the rotten food was _____.

18. Mixing certain chemical substances can produce _____ fumes.

19. "Yes," Gillian agreed. "Marcus's joke was _____."

20. "I can't eat with him; his table manners are so _____!" exclaimed Daisy.

How well did you do?   Total Score: _____ / 20

#33 Bygone Days

A. About these words...

All the words in this week's list are ones that you might encounter when reading about **various types of societies** and **governments in history**.

B. Head Count...

Have a look at the questions below. Then, read all of this week's target words carefully. Once you've done that, come back and answer these questions.

How many of these words do you **sort of know**? _____

How many of these words do you **definitely know**? _____

How many of these words **haven't you seen before**? _____

C. The Top 5...

Before you start learning these words, make a note here of the **five** that you think are the **most predictable** to be included:

_____

_____

_____

_____

_____

Why have you chosen these five words?

HOMONYM HASSLE

The noun **sovereign** means ruler, but it also refers to a British gold coin that used to be worth £1.

This Week's Target Words!

annals	legislature
antiquity	monarchy
aristocracy	patriarch
bourgeoisie	peasantry
chronological	prehistoric
civil war	rebellion
constitution	republic
democracy	sovereign
documentation	testament
epoch	tyranny

VOCABULARY BUILDER

This list contains several groups of words that are connected to each other:

- **Social classes**: aristocracy | bourgeoisie | peasantry
- **Forms of government**: democracy | monarchy | republic | tyranny
- **Time-related words**: antiquity | chronological | epoch | prehistoric

Can you see any other connections? *(Clue: rulers)*

POWER SPELLER'S TIP

Four words in this list contain the **tricky letter string 'ch'** which is pronounced **'k'**:

chronological | epo**ch**

monar**ch**y | patriar**ch**

PRONUNCIATION PUZZLE

The noun **bourgeoisie** can be a tricky word to pronounce because it is a French loanword.

One way to pronounce it is to say it as if it were spelled

boar + jwa + zee

TEST #33: Think you've mastered your words for the week? If so, carry on!

1. "These letters provide interesting insights into the _____," noted the historian.

2. Some people think Shakespeare's history plays are best read in _____ order.

3. In geology, an '_____' is a unit of time greater than an 'age', but less than a 'period'.

4. In 1381, the English _____ revolted against the imposition of new taxes.

5. After the assassination of Julius Caesar, the Romans descended into _____.

6. The first work by Plato that I read was *The* _____.

7. Renaissance paintings are a _____ to the cultural impact of ancient Greek myths.

8. The worship of multiple gods and goddesses was common in _____.

9. The removal of the _____ enabled the army to seize control of the country.

10. "The proposed changes to their _____ are sure to ignite debate," observed Ada.

11. "The available _____ does not support your claim," argued the scholar.

12. At the time of his death, the tribe's _____ had ruled for forty years.

13. *The* _____ is a work by Tacitus that charts the history of the Roman Empire.

14. "We must do everything we can to preserve our _____!" declared the politician.

15. In many countries, the _____ is called the National Assembly.

16. During the French Revolution, members of the _____ were executed on the guillotine.

17. Our local museum boasts an impressive collection of _____ tools.

18. '_____' can be used to mean 'middle class'.

19. Queen Elizabeth II is currently the UK's longest-reigning _____.

20. Over the centuries, many philosophers have written treatises on the subject of _____.

How well did you do?   Total Score: _____ / 20

#34 Out-
The Outnumbered

This Week's Target Words!

outbreak	outperformed
outburst	outpouring
outcome	output
outflanked	outreach
outgunned	outskirts
outlast	outsourced
outliers	outstay
outmaneuvers	outstretched
outnumber	outweigh
outpace	outwit

VOCABULARY BUILDER

This list contains several groups of words that are linked to each other:

- **Soldier-related words**: outflanked | outgunned | outmaneuvers | outnumber
- **Margin-related words**: outliers | outskirts

Can you see any other words that are linked in this list? *(Clue: emotions)*

WORD NERD FACTS

Although we might think that the word **outlier** is a relatively recent one, its first use actually dates back to the **beginning of the seventeenth century**!

In fact, **only two words** in this list are **twentieth-century words**:

outperform

outsource

A. About these words...

This week's words are all ones that can take the **prefix 'out-'** at their beginnings.

Using this prefix adds the sense of **'in a way that surpasses or exceeds'** to a word.

B. Head Count...

Have a look at the questions below. Then, read all of this week's target words carefully. Once you've done that, come back and answer these questions.

How many of these words do you **sometimes use**? _____

How many of these words do you **often use**? _____

How many of these words do you **never use**? _____

C. The Top 5...

Before you start learning these words, make a note here of the **five** that you think you will find the **easiest** to remember:

_____

_____

_____

_____

_____

Why do you think these five words will be the least challenging for you to learn?

CHEAT CODE!

As with the other lists of words that contain prefixes, once you've **mastered the specific prefix**, you can **concentrate on the second halves of the words**.

TEST #34: See how many words you've got the hang of this week!

1. Try as he might, Rick could not _____ his sister.

2. "What unites these companies is the fact that they are _____," said the economist.

3. The school had to be closed following an _____ of chicken pox.

4. In exams, Nat has always _____ most of his peers.

5. My cousin Edna has just started working at an _____ center for the homeless.

6. When the attack came from behind, the soldiers realized they'd been _____.

7. There was an _____ of support for the victims of the earthquake.

8. Some of this work will have to be _____; there's too much here for us to do.

9. "I'm always worried that I will _____ my welcome," admitted Marianne.

10. This year's election is very close; it is impossible to predict the _____.

11. The little boy ran to his mother's _____ arms.

12. In our class, the girls _____ the boys by two to one.

13. Under the circumstances, Ivan's angry _____ was entirely predictable.

14. Last year, the factory's _____ dropped by roughly twenty percent.

15. I never play chess with Brad; he always completely _____ me.

16. Odysseus came up with a cunning plan to _____ the Trojans.

17. "Your legacy, sire, will _____ us all," the vizier promised the sultan.

18. The sheriff and his men found themselves _____ by the outlaws.

19. "I think the benefits of this plan _____ its risks," agreed Cecile.

20. "The well that you seek lies on the _____ of the village of Arden," said the witch.

How well did you do?   Total Score: _____ / 20

#35 The Silver Screen

A. About these words...

All this week's words are ones that you might come across when you're reading about **the engrossing world of cinema, movies, and factual films**.

B. Head Count...

Have a look at the questions below. Then, read all of this week's target words carefully. Once you've done that, come back and answer these questions.

How many of these words do you *definitely know*? _____

How many of these words *haven't you seen before*? _____

How many of these words do you *sort of know*? _____

C. The Top 5...

Before you start learning these words, make a note here of the **five** that you find the **most interesting**:

_____

_____

_____

_____

_____

Why do you think these five words appeal to you?

BRILLIANT BREAKDOWN

Break down long words into smaller units:

choreographers: ch•o•re•o•gra•ph•ers

This Week's Target Words!

animated	franchise
audience	freeze-frames
audio description	intermission
auditorium	location
biopic	premiere
choreographers	release
clips	screenplay
computer-generated	scriptwriter
documentary	subtitles
footage	trailer

VOCABULARY BUILDER

This list contains several groups of words that are connected to each other:

- **Words also related to video games**: animated | computer-generated | franchise | release | trailer
- **Words related to factual films**: biopic | documentary | footage | subtitles

Can you come up with any more groups? *(Clue: extracts or parts of movies)*

HOMONYM HASSLE

As well as meaning a selection of scenes from a movie or program, the word **trailer** can refer to several other things.

One of these is **a cart that carries small loads that can be attached to the back of a vehicle**.

D. Notable Mnemonic...

P-R-E-M-I-E-R-E

Penguins **r**egard **e**agles **m**ost **i**nsolently, **e**specially **r**oyal **e**agles.

Now try coming up with one of your own!

TEST #35: Feeling certain that you know your weekly words? If so, dive right in!

1. "That _____ is terrible; it's full of spoilers!" complained Wendy.

2. The use of _____ imagery is now a staple of filmmaking.

3. The _____ argued long and hard over the changes the producers wanted to make.

4. The studio is set to announce the date for the _____ of its latest blockbuster.

5. "I saw several _____ from that movie on TV," Lionel said.

6. "I can't name my favorite _____ cartoon; there are too many!" laughed Carlos.

7. "I found this movie's use of actual war _____ very moving," said the critic.

8. Some members of the _____ complained that the sound was too loud.

9. It is now odd to think that, in theaters, movies were once shown with an _____.

10. Apparently, a new _____ about Elvis Presley has gone into production.

11. Her office walls were covered with _____ from the movies she'd worked on.

12. Their latest _____ has been nominated for several awards.

13. Disappointingly, the _____ of the movie has been delayed again.

14. In the future, we want _____ for customers to be the norm, not the exception.

15. Can you name five influential _____ of the twentieth century?

16. Every film studio dreams of coming up with the next big _____.

17. As the movie reached its terrifying climax, the _____ was completely silent.

18. "Is this Italian movie available with English _____?" the customer asked.

19. That director's movies are always filmed on _____ in Canada.

20. Deservedly, the movie won the Oscar for Best Original _____.

How well did you do? Total Score: _____ / 20

#36 City Central

A. About these words...

All this week's words end with the **suffix '-ity'**.

This is yet another suffix which, when added to words, **forms nouns**.

B. Head Count...

Have a look at the questions below. Then, read all of this week's target words carefully. Once you've done that, come back and answer these questions.

How many of these words do you *sort of know*? _____

How many of these words do you *definitely know*? _____

How many of these words *haven't you seen before*? _____

C. The Top 5...

Before you start learning these words, make a note here of the **five** that are your **least favorite**:

_____

_____

_____

_____

_____

Why don't you like these five words?

PRONUNCIATION PUZZLE

The 'au' in **audacity, authenticity,** and, **paucity** should be pronounced as if they were spelled *awe*.

This Week's Target Words!

atrocity	multiplicity
audacity	opacity
authenticity	paucity
complicity	reciprocity
domesticity	scarcity
duplicity	synchronicity
eccentricity	tenacity
egocentricity	toxicity
ferocity	veracity
incapacity	vivacity

SYNONYM & ANTONYM SOUP

This list contains two pairs of synonyms:

- authenticity = veracity
- scarcity = paucity

It also contains an antonym pair:

- authenticity ≠ duplicity

Can you think of any synonyms or antonyms of your own for other words in your list?

VOCABULARY BUILDER

This list contains several groups of related words:

- **Negative Character Traits**: duplicity | egocentricity
- **Positive Character Traits**: authenticity | tenacity | vivacity

Can you come up with any more groups? *(Clue: violence)*

D. Notable Mnemonic...

A-U-D-A-C-I-T-Y

Alan **u**nderestimated **D**ave **a**nd **C**arol's **i**nclination **t**o **y**ammer.

Now try coming up with one of your own!

TEST #36: Positive that you're now an expert on this week's words? Then wait no longer!

1. "The _____ level of the soil is regularly checked," said the scientist.

2. Vera's cheerfulness and _____ made her extremely popular at work.

3. The spy's _____ resulted in many state secrets being shared with the enemy.

4. People are outraged by this _____.

5. The _____ of Linus's denial took Paulina by surprise.

6. "Given the _____ of evidence, it is impossible to arrive at a conclusion," Jo noted.

7. Police officers have arrested a man for suspected _____ in the heist.

8. It took Angelica hours to check the _____ of the information in her article.

9. The ballet dancers gave a performance that was perfect in its _____.

10. Sadly, some of Pete's neighbors were not very tolerant of his _____.

11. The opposite of 'transparency' is '_____'.

12. I find her _____ to take responsibility for her mistakes infuriating.

13. The _____ of the painting has been questioned by an art historian.

14. The increasing _____ of many species is a cause for genuine concern.

15. "I can't believe Bob had the _____ to take my phone without asking!" fumed Otto.

16. The king's growing _____ began to make him unpopular with his people.

17. Many advertisements use scenes of comfortable _____ to promote products.

18. "The _____ of this stain is really annoying; it won't come out," grumbled Mark.

19. The narrative is very rich and is thus open to a _____ of interpretations.

20. One example of '_____' is when two people help each other.

How well did you do?   Total Score: _____ / 20

#37 Bookish Business

This Week's Target Words!

allegories
anecdote
appendix
dedication
encyclopedia
epigraph
epilogue
footnotes
foreshadows
glossary

index
pagination
parody
perspective
plagiarism
preface
prologue
protagonist
satire
thesaurus

VOCABULARY BUILDER

This list contains at least one large group of words that are closely connected:

- **Parts of books**: appendix | dedication | epigraph | epilogue | footnotes | glossary | index | preface | prologue

Can you see any other connections between words in this list? *(Clue: reference books)*

ANTONYM ALERT

This list contains an antonym pair:

- prologue ≠ epilogue

Can you think of any antonyms of your own for other words in the list?

BRILLIANT BREAKDOWNS

Breaking down long words into smaller units can help you remember them:

appendix: ap•pen•di•x
encyclopedia: en•cy•clo•pe•di•a
protagonist: pro•ta•gon•ist

A. About these words...

The words in the list this week are a mixture of words to do with **types of books** and words for **particular parts of books**.

TIP: If any of these words are unfamiliar to you, do look them up in your dictionary.

B. Head Count...

Have a look at the questions below. Then, read all of this week's target words carefully. Once you've done that, come back and answer these questions.

How many of these words do you **never use**? _____

How many of these words do you **often use**? _____

How many of these words do you **sometimes use**? _____

C. The Top 5...

Before you start learning these words, make a note here of the **five** you think you will find the **most useful** to you in your writing:

_____

_____

_____

_____

_____

How do you think using these five words will help you?

POWER SPELLER'S TIP

The word **encyclopedia** can also be correctly spelled in British English as **encyclopaedia** (i.e. **with the first 'a'**).

TEST #37: Feeling confident you've learned this week's words? Then give this test a go!

1. No longer used, the _____ sat on the top shelf gathering dust.

2. Further illustrative tables can be found in the book's _____.

3. That book needs a _____; it's full of words I've never seen before.

4. One possible use of a _____ is to pique the audience's curiosity.

5. "The _____ to the author's father is incredibly moving," said Eve.

6. '_____' is stealing someone else's work and pretending that it's yours.

7. As Indira loves words, she spends hours reading entries in her _____.

8. I've just discovered *Bored of the Rings*: a _____ of Tolkien's *Lord of the Rings* trilogy.

9. The _____ in this document is incorrect; it jumps from page five to page ten.

10. You are far more likely to find _____ in a scholarly work than in a novel.

11. Unusually, the story is told from the _____ of the hero's horse.

12. _____ are often used by writers as a way of talking about controversial ideas.

13. The autobiography began with an _____ from the writer's childhood.

14. To write an effective _____, you need to understand the work you are criticizing.

15. A book's _____ is to be found at its beginning.

16. The death of a dog _____ the death of the main character later on.

17. It's impossible to find anything in that book; it doesn't have an _____.

18. "That novel's _____ didn't work; it didn't relate to the story at all," Keira said.

19. '_____' is a single word that means 'main character'.

20. "Why are you reading the book's _____ first?" Max asked in amazement.

How well did you do? Total Score: _____ / 20

#38 The Big Top

This Week's Target Words!

acrobatic	juggler
admission	ringmaster
aerialist	sequins
audaciously	snake charmer
contortionist	somersaulting
death-defying	stilts
fascination	sword-swallower
fire-eater	trampoline
hippodromes	trapeze
hula hooper	troupe

VOCABULARY BUILDER

Not surprisingly, this list contains quite a lot of words that are closely linked:

- **Performers at a circus**: aerialist | contortionist | fire-eater | hula hooper | juggler | ringmaster | snake charmer | sword-swallower

Can you think of any more groups? *(Clue: gymnastics)*

HOMOPHONE HUNT

Remember not to confuse the word **troupe** with its homophone **troop**!

D. Notable Mnemonic...

T-R-A-P-E-Z-E

Tina **r**ewrote **a**nd **p**osted **e**leven **z**any **e**xercises.

Now try coming up with one of your own!

A. About these words...

The words in this week's list are all ones that are connected to **the mesmerizing world of the circus**.

B. Head Count...

Have a look at the questions below. Then, read all of this week's target words carefully. Once you've done that, come back and answer these questions.

How many of these words do you **often use**? _____

How many of these words do you **sometimes use**? _____

How many of these words do you **never use**? _____

C. The Top 5...

Before you start learning these words, make a note here of the **five** that you are **least surprised** to find in the list:

_____

_____

_____

_____

_____

Why do you think these five words were most likely to be included here?

WORD NERD FACT

The word **hippodrome(s)** comes from two Greek words: *hippos*, meaning 'horse' and *dromos*, meaning 'course'.

TEST #38: Find out how well you remember this week's words!

1. As the performers took their places, the kids gazed on in rapt _____.

2. "Look! That poster says the _____ performs blindfolded!" Rick said excitedly.

3. Bouncing up and down on the _____, the clowns kept trying to push one another off.

4. _____ were originally ancient Greek stadiums used for horse and chariot races.

5. I've always wanted to try walking on _____, but I'm scared of heights.

6. With _____ bravery, the young girl stepped onto the tightrope.

7. _____, the clown crept up behind the magician and grabbed his hat.

8. Everyone gasped as the _____ twisted into a seemingly impossible shape.

9. The spellbinding feats of the _____ left her audience breathless.

10. The performers that the twins most enjoyed were the _____ clowns.

11. "It must take hours to sew all those _____ onto those costumes," observed Sula.

12. "The cost of _____ for children under twelve is $5," read the sign.

13. "I can't watch!" squeaked Zeinab as the _____ draped a python round his neck.

14. When he went to the circus, Tommy was captivated by the _____.

15. A _____ is a performer who passes a long blade down their throat into their stomach.

16. As the _____ stepped out before the crowd, all the lights went off save one.

17. "The performance I most want to see is that of the _____," confided Amy.

18. "I thought the _____ artists were particularly mesmerizing," said Lucy.

19. The kids laughed at the antics of the _____ of mischievous monkeys.

20. We were enthralled by the stunning _____ feats taking place high above us.

How well did you do? Total Score: _____ / 20

#39 That's a Proper Word?!?!

A. About these words...

Believe it or not, all the words in this final list are **actually proper words**...

B. Head Count...

Have a look at the questions below. Then, read all of this week's target words carefully. Once you've done that, come back and answer these questions.

How many of these words **haven't you seen before**? _____

How many of these words do you **sort of know**? _____

How many of these words do you **definitely know**? _____

C. The Top 5...

Before you start learning these words, make a note here of the **five** that you think are the **most fun**:

_____

_____

_____

_____

_____

Why do you think you find these five words the most entertaining?

D. Notable Mnemonic...

A-M-O-K
Alice's **m**other **o**ffended **K**elly.

This Week's Target Words!

agog	fiddlesticks
amok	genteel
balderdash	gizmo
bamboozled	heyday
bedlam	hogwash
cahoots	huzzahs
desperadoes	ignoramus
didgeridoo	ironclad
doldrums	jalopy
fez	jamboree

SYNONYM SPOTTING

It's quite hard to find synonyms within this list, but there is one pair!

- balderdash = hogwash

Can you think of any synonyms of your own for words in the list?

WORD NERD FACT

The word **didgeridoo** is an onomatopoeic word from an Australian Aboriginal language.

It refers to a musical instrument whose sound it imitates.

POWER SPELLER'S TIP

The word **amok** can also be correctly spelled **amuck**.

BRILLIANT BREAKDOWNS

Breaking down long words into smaller units can help you remember them:

balderdash: bald•er•dash
doldrums: dol•drums
jamboree: jam•bo•ree

TEST #39: Think you've mastered your words for the week? If so, for the last time, carry on!

1. "Oh, _____!" said Cordelia crossly. "I've burnt my toast again."

2. "I know you love your _____, but isn't it time you bought a new car?" Arvind asked.

3. "Don't call your brother an _____!" scolded Vicki's mother.

4. Although it had seen better days, the mansion retained an air of _____ elegance.

5. As more people arrived, our lawn party turned into a fully-fledged _____.

6. In their _____, that boy band sold more tickets than any other group.

7. Some dishonest caller _____ my grandpa into giving them fifty dollars.

8. Ursula is researching accounts of infamous nineteenth-century _____.

9. We were all _____, waiting to see what would happen next.

10. My friend Sookie was in the _____, so I went round to try to cheer her up.

11. "I know the truth: I know that you and Jane are in _____," stated Freddy.

12. The mayor and his wife were greeted by loud _____ and clapping.

13. "That is completely untrue! Utter _____!" spluttered Brian.

14. It's impossible to get a sensible answer out of Julian; he spouts nothing but _____.

15. Played by Australian Aborigines, the _____ is a long, wooden wind instrument.

16. "I've got an _____ alibi," the suspect smugly told the detective.

17. The authorities warned the protesters that they would not be allowed to run _____.

18. The family lunch descended into _____ when a fire started in the kitchen.

19. "I have no idea how to work this _____!" grumbled Jorge irritably.

20. In the old portrait stood a distinguished, middle-aged gentleman wearing a _____.

How well did you do? Total Score: _____ / 20

NOTES FOR PARENTS & TEACHERS

The Spelling Tests Transcripts

On the following pages (pp. 84-103), you will find the complete transcripts for the 39 spelling tests in this workbook. Each transcript consists of the 20 sentences included in its respective test, complete with the missing target spelling marked in bold. For example, if a target spelling were the word '**playground**', you would find a sentence like the one below in the test transcript:

10. The **playground** was full of laughing children.

Suggestions for Administering the Spelling Tests

How you administer the tests is up to you, but you might find the following suggestions useful:

Option 1:
- Read out the sentence along with the missing word, saying aloud: *The playground was full of laughing children*

Option 2:
- Read out the target spelling first, saying aloud: *Playground*
- Wait for a few seconds
- Then read out the whole sentence, saying aloud: *The playground was full of laughing children*

Option 3:
- Start with a brief statement like: *Spelling Number 10 is playground*, or, *Number 10 is playground*, or, *The word is playground*
- Wait for a few seconds
- Then read out the whole sentence, saying aloud: *The playground was full of laughing children*

Suggestions for Timing & Grading the Spelling Tests

It is entirely up to you how much time you wish to give your child to do the tests. You may wish to remove the time factor so that they feel less anxious or pressured. Alternatively, you may want to make the spelling tests a bit of a challenge, in which case, set a time limit (e.g. fifteen minutes) that you feel is appropriate for your child.

Each test carries **a maximum score of 20**. However, **how to award points is also left to your discretion**. You may wish to award 1 point for each correct answer and 0 points for any incorrect answers. Alternatively, to encourage your child, you might want to award half points in some instances; for example, when a word is spelled correctly, but is missing a necessary capital letter.

GOOD LUCK!

SPELLING TESTS TRANSCRIPTS

Spelling Test #1

1. The free, plastic toy that comes with those cereals is just a marketing **gimmick**.
2. "Cool" is one of my least favorite **colloquial** terms.
3. In protest at recent events, many **ambassadors** have been recalled from that country.
4. Students and teachers alike have complained that the **syllabus** is too long.
5. Dr. Dee's shelves held many books that dealt with the **occult**.
6. Lucinda gave **utterance** to what we were all thinking, but couldn't say.
7. For years, this **territory** has been a source of tension in the region.
8. The charm of this design lies in its lack of **symmetry**.
9. The conference **attendees** were told to gather in the hotel's lobby.
10. "These results must be **erroneous**; they make no sense," the scientist declared.
11. I am extremely **attached** to my old jeans; I've traveled everywhere in them.
12. The **efficacy** of this new cure is being debated by the medical profession.
13. Nat wants to get a **tattoo**, but his mother keeps refusing to let him.
14. That spacious SUV can **accommodate** up to eight passengers.
15. The drachma used to be the **currency** of Greece before the euro was introduced.
16. The **essence** of Keyla's argument is that she thinks we're right.
17. Jordan has just **accused** me of losing our train tickets.
18. Petronella wondered at the costly **apparel** of the king's guests.
19. The government is issuing regular **bulletins** to keep us updated.
20. If the device is no longer under **warranty**, I'm afraid I can't fix it.

Spelling Test #2

1. Professor Moriarty, Sherlock Holmes's **nemesis**, gave a long, low laugh.
2. Lilly and Lola managed to resolve their differences **amicably**.
3. Despite their rivalry, the two teams have a **cordial** relationship with each other.
4. The **camaraderie** among the soldiers was plain for all to see.
5. Jim and his **crony**, Bob, are planning to gate-crash the party.
6. The courageous knight charged into the thick of the **fray**.
7. We thanked our hosts for creating such a **genial** atmosphere.
8. The young elf was **befriended** by a group of gnomes.
9. In a **tussle** between Batman and Spider-Man, who would win?
10. I've never seen Uncle Ewan in such a **jovial** mood; he can't stop smiling!
11. A small group of soldiers made a lightning **foray** into the enemy camp.
12. "How very **neighborly** of you to help me, dear!" said the old lady gratefully.
13. Jack and Jill are **inseparable**; they go everywhere together.
14. Several people were hurt in the **melee** that broke out near the stadium.
15. The debate between the two candidates descended into an undignified **dogfight**.
16. Unnamed **saboteurs** are being blamed for the factory explosion.
17. Before the fight began, the **combatants** sized each other up.
18. Angela is such an **affable** person; she's so easy to talk to!
19. Reports are coming in of a **skirmish** along the border.
20. Olivia defeated her old **adversary**, Viola, in the semifinals.

Spelling Test #3

1. The current **implications** are that the culprit will soon be apprehended.
2. The psychiatrist's **testimony** greatly influenced the jury's verdict.
3. In *The Sign of Four*, Sherlock Holmes's **investigative** skills are stretched to the limit.
4. Al Capone is possibly one of the most famous **gangsters** of the twentieth century.
5. Mr. Jacobs hired a **private investigator** to look into his business rival's activities.
6. The moral of the story is that **villainy** is always punished.
7. Government agents installed a **wiretap** on the suspect's phone.
8. Unfortunately, Ron was a **victim** of identity theft last year.
9. The **criminal underworld** has been rocked by the arrest of its most notorious member.
10. After several weeks of **shadowing** Mrs. Green, I decided she was innocent.
11. Over the years, Hollywood has released innumerable **mafia** movies.
12. He discovered he had been under police **surveillance** for six months.
13. It does not take much **deduction** to work out who ate all the pie.
14. The **mobsters** threatened to harm Pierre's family if he did not cooperate.
15. Our **suspicions** that our system was hacked have now been confirmed.
16. TV **sleuths** lead far more exciting lives than their real-life counterparts.
17. The **informant** waited nervously under the bridge in the dark.
18. "We've received **intelligence** that will help us crack the case," the captain stated.
19. Mrs. Singh **witnessed** her neighbor's car being vandalized.
20. The recent developments in **forensics** are mind-boggling.

Spelling Test #4

1. "I don't actually like scrambled eggs," Melinda **confessed** to me.
2. "Please, let us stay up to watch the game!" **begged** Linus and Lionel.
3. "Don't hurt me!" the cowardly lion **beseeched** the mouse.
4. "Move the siege towers into position," **commanded** Atticus, the Roman general.
5. "I've just bought the latest iPhone," Francis **bragged**.
6. "Could you bring me some more water?" **requested** the customer.
7. "You should never, EVER do that again!" **lectured** my mother.
8. "My head hurts; I've got a headache," **moaned** Billy.
9. "I'm telling you that I don't know!" Tim **reiterated** irritably.
10. "But what did you see?!" **interrupted** Davina.
11. "I was the one who broke the vase," Nancy finally **admitted**.
12. "Don't be angry with me," **pleaded** Rachel.
13. "Never go into the woods at night," the old woman **warned** the young boy.
14. "I haven't the faintest idea," **responded** Candy.
15. "Why do I have to do Jenny's shopping for her?" **grumbled** Ruth.
16. "This project must be completed by the end of the month," **instructed** the boss.
17. "Where," **interrogated** the FBI agent, "were you last Tuesday at midnight?"
18. "Honesty," Rose **preached** primly, "is always the best policy."
19. "I don't believe that for a second," **retorted** Geoff.
20. "What a wonderful surprise!" **exclaimed** Hilda delightedly.

Spelling Test #5

1. By the end of the tragedy, Lady Macbeth has become completely **unhinged**.
2. Yolanda's outfit was utterly **unsuited** to the occasion.
3. My mum has an **unerring** ability to tell when I'm lying.
4. Thankfully, everyone emerged **unscathed** from the accident.
5. That man bears an **uncanny** resemblance to my grandfather.
6. An **unnamed** informant was the source of the tip-off.
7. "What's in here?" grumbled Pete. "I've never carried such an **unwieldy** suitcase before!"
8. The sorceress's warnings went **unheeded** by the stubborn villagers.
9. The government believes there are **untapped** mineral resources in this remote region.
10. A jury is supposed to remain **unbiased** while hearing the evidence.
11. Our attempts to **unravel** the mystery of the missing manuscript have failed so far.
12. "How **uncouth** of him to turn his back on you!" exclaimed Aisha to Eva.
13. We watched as the sails of the schooner were gradually **unfurled**.
14. Maria wrinkled her nose in disgust at the **unsavory** smells coming from the trash can.
15. As they sailed away, the crew knew they were entering **uncharted** waters.
16. Ross exploded with **unbridled** fury when he heard the news.
17. "We're hoping to **unearth** valuable artifacts," the archaeologist told the reporter.
18. "If the king's greed remains **unchecked**, we shall all suffer," cautioned Merlin.
19. The continued silence began to **unnerve** the audience.
20. The rumors of the company's collapse are entirely **unfounded**.

Spelling Test #6

1. "The accusation that I am the murderer is **preposterous**!" fumed Lord Godolphin.
2. Bridget could not explain the **irrational** fear that suddenly hit her.
3. It was very hard indeed not to laugh at their **risible** comments.
4. "It is **foolhardy** to think that you can defeat the mage," Tayla told the apprentice.
5. "I think his tale is too **far-fetched** to be true," commented Ricardo.
6. Juno specializes in **ridiculous** suggestions; she is so impractical!
7. "I really want to call her **asinine**, but that would be rude," Tania said.
8. It is **unreasonable** for you to expect me to read a thousand-page novel in one day.
9. "What **harebrained** scheme has the mad professor come up with now?" asked Yasmina.
10. The more **outrageous** the suggestion, the more likely it is that people will talk about it.
11. "Offering to help once the damage is done is simply **inane**," Indira pointed out.
12. The politician's obvious attempts to lie were **farcical**.
13. The plot of that movie was **ludicrous**; it was completely unbelievable.
14. We were appalled by the **senseless** destruction of the ancient temple.
15. "You can't fix a broken window with glue; that's just **idiotic**," scoffed Vera.
16. "It would be **irresponsible** of me not to warn you of the dangers," Sam said gravely.
17. "That is the most **absurd** idea I've ever heard," said Fred in disgust.
18. "You haven't been listening at all; your comments are totally **nonsensical**," complained Willa.
19. "Putting salt in coffee," Pip said to me, "is a **balmy** notion."
20. "Your **frivolous** attitude to the problem is inappropriate," scolded Jan.

Spelling Test #7

1. Having brought down a young impala, the cheetah proceeded to **devour** it.
2. **Exhausted** by the chase, the zebra sank to the ground.
3. Under cover of darkness, the wolves **prowled** the village streets.
4. Having identified its next meal, the eagle **swooped** down to make its kill.
5. Not all **predators** are large creatures; they can be as small as the net-casting spider.
6. An **omnivore** is a creature that eats both meat and plants.
7. With infinite care, the tiger began to **stalk** through the long grass.
8. I find the **butchering** of wild animals by poachers deeply distressing.
9. The young gazelle was **ambushed** by three lionesses.
10. The **corpse** of a victim of a shark attack washed up on the beach.
11. Most big cats are solitary creatures and hunt their **quarry** alone.
12. Disa stopped watching the wildlife documentary; the **bloodshed** was too much for her.
13. The hunter carefully set up a series of rabbit **snares**.
14. There are reports of **feral** hogs causing serious damage to crops in Alabama.
15. Local people are hunting a man-eating tiger which has left a string of **cadavers** in its wake.
16. **Carrion** birds are birds that feed on the dead flesh of other birds or animals.
17. Coyotes will **prey** on a wide range of things, including insects and snakes.
18. Vultures circled the elephant's **carcass**.
19. Hyenas are some of the animal kingdom's most well-known **scavengers**.
20. As the pride of lions moved on, smaller creatures emerged to feast on the **carnage**.

Spelling Test #8

1. The train **wreckage** is being searched for survivors.
2. Catherine can trace her **lineage** back to the reign of George III.
3. **Sabotage** may have caused the plane crash.
4. This antique writing desk is a prized part of our family **heritage**.
5. The hero of the novel I'm reading grew up in an **orphanage**.
6. "Could you explain what **stoppage** time is?" Misha asked.
7. If we were all a bit more careful, we could drastically reduce global food **wastage**.
8. The media's **coverage** of this election has been relentless.
9. A car's **mileage** is one factor that affects its resale value.
10. The **seepage** from these old batteries has ruined the remote control.
11. During the Renaissance, **patronage** was one way for artists to earn money.
12. High-**voltage** fences have been erected around the chemical plant.
13. Under the philosopher's **tutelage**, the young princess acquired much wisdom.
14. The soles of these boots are designed to prevent **slippage**.
15. Avoid unwanted **spillage** by firmly tightening the cap on the bottle.
16. I've taken out insurance for my phone to cover screen **breakage**.
17. "Do you know what **percentage** of the population buys newspapers?" Andy asked.
18. Graceland is a popular **pilgrimage** destination for Elvis Presley fans.
19. "How much **storage** space has your new laptop got?" Ben inquired.
20. An efficient **drainage** system is a key element of public sanitation.

Spelling Test #9

1. The field was filled with the sound of **droning** bees.
2. Surprisingly, the slight elf had a deep, reassuringly **sonorous** voice.
3. A group of **ululating** women had gathered outside the bride's home.
4. Bruce's **resonant** "Silence!" stopped us all in our tracks.
5. Rhoda was kept awake by a **caterwauling** animal in her backyard.
6. The birds were quite **raucous** as they squabbled over the crumbs.
7. Two of Tina's favorite **rhythmic** dances are the rumba and the mambo.
8. In a round, several voices begin singing at different points, yet remain **harmonious**.
9. The diner's kitchen was filled with the sound of **clattering** dishes.
10. A **tumultuous** crash outside the house brought us all running to investigate.
11. The **dulcet** tones of the choir could be heard outside the church.
12. **Blaring** music was coming from our neighbor's outdoor speakers.
13. The **ricocheting** echoes in the cave were quite disorienting.
14. Some contemporary classical music can be quite **discordant**.
15. I've always found playing **staccato** notes a bit of a challenge.
16. Many composers have produced both **symphonic** works and chamber music.
17. A worrying, **monotonous** thudding started coming from the dishwasher.
18. The mother's low, **mellifluous** voice lulled her child to sleep.
19. Heavy metal concerts are nothing if not **cacophonous**.
20. The **plaintive** mewling of the abandoned kittens was heartbreaking.

Spelling Test #10

1. Seeing his enemy approach, Sir Galahad readied his **lance**.
2. The arrival of a wandering **troubadour** filled the villagers with excitement.
3. In the Middle Ages, **parchment** was made from the skin of calves, lambs, or goats.
4. Some of the most famous **tournament** fields were located in northeastern France.
5. The **longbow** was favored by English archers.
6. Barry has quite an unusual hobby: the study of **heraldry**.
7. The Bayeux **Tapestry** is currently in a museum in Normandy, France.
8. "The **chronicles** are silent on the fate of King Stefan the Swift," the sorceress noted.
9. "Summon the court **jester**," ordered the king. "I wish to be entertained."
10. Exhausted by the fight, the rebel finally lowered his **broadsword** and surrendered.
11. The precise dates of the **medieval** period are often debated by scholars.
12. The traitors' heads were displayed on the castle's **ramparts** as a grim warning.
13. The travelers could see colorful **pennants** adorning the castle's battlements.
14. One of the most powerful **fiefs** in Gascony, France, was the county of Armagnac.
15. "How common was **pillaging** in the Middle Ages?" the student asked.
16. The Black Death, or the **Plague**, devastated countless populations.
17. In a **chivalrous** act, Sir Tristan gave his last hunk of bread to the starving child.
18. The **catapult** was a weapon often used during sieges in the Middle Ages.
19. Certain aspects of **guilds** in the Middle Ages resemble modern-day trade unions.
20. '**Feudalism**' is not a term that was used in the Middle Ages; it was formulated later on.

Spelling Test #11

1. "No," replied Nancy, with unusual **bluntness**.
2. The **scantiness** of evidence is hindering the investigation.
3. With swift **deftness**, the tailor mended the gaping hole in the young man's coat.
4. Although this book is rather strange, I've really enjoyed its **quirkiness**.
5. Princess Flora was famed throughout the land for her **comeliness**.
6. "Our **indebtedness** to you shall be eternal," the grateful villagers told the elves.
7. A strange **haziness** surrounded the ship on the horizon.
8. Staring at the chaos, Gina could not believe Ellie's **ineptness** at filing.
9. Notwithstanding the **foreignness** of the spices it contained, the casserole was delicious.
10. He found the **weightiness** of the decision too much to bear alone.
11. Our anxiety resulted in several nights of **wakefulness**.
12. You could argue that it is Romeo's **callowness** that causes the tragedy.
13. The **steeliness** of my father's frown stopped me in my tracks.
14. "Sanjeev's **haughtiness** will be his downfall," predicted Xavier.
15. After Wanda left, her footsteps gradually faded into **nothingness**.
16. The lost children felt their hunger with an indescribable **keenness**.
17. The **adroitness** with which the politician changed the subject was remarkable.
18. Keira loves **exactness**; however, this does have its drawbacks.
19. A think tank has questioned the **robustness** of the inquiry.
20. You should never underestimate the **shrewdness** of successful politicians.

Spelling Test #12

1. As the storm grew, the waves became increasingly **turbulent**.
2. Thankfully, we have had a **bountiful** harvest this year.
3. You can't use that photo, the image is too **distorted**.
4. The **searing** heat of the sun beat down on them relentlessly.
5. "Could you please leave the door **ajar** on your way out?" Sandy asked.
6. It was impossible to see anything through the shed's **opaque** windows.
7. In the middle of the forest, they found a delightful **canopied** clearing.
8. "Your hands are really **grimy**! What have you been up to?" Tim's sister asked him.
9. The makers of this video game have created an impressively **immersive** environment.
10. The **grandiose** interior of the palace was stunning.
11. "You don't scare me!" the **feisty** fairy told the ogre.
12. "I'm not paying all that for a purse; that's **exorbitant**!" snorted Lisa.
13. A set of **grotesque** gargoyles adorned the building's exterior.
14. The narrow tunnel suddenly gave way to a **cavernous** chamber full of treasure.
15. The **intrepid** adventurer decided to explore a remote part of the island.
16. Roy's study is **spartan** because he can't stand clutter.
17. When I broke my ankle, the pain was **excruciating**.
18. After so much cheering during the game, Kim found she had become quite **hoarse**.
19. The **avaricious** accountant swindled several of his clients out of their savings.
20. The shed was full of rusty, **antiquated** machinery that was unusable.

Spelling Test #13

1. The grouchy old woman was well-known for her **ill-natured** remarks.
2. The only response I got from George was an **ill-humored** grunt.
3. The *Bellerophon*'s **ill-omened** voyage began on December 28, 1876.
4. The plan to attack in the dark was **ill-considered**; the troops couldn't see a thing.
5. A person who doesn't enjoy reading is **ill-suited** to the study of literature.
6. The large, **ill-tempered** ogre muttered angrily to himself as he stomped away.
7. The campers realized they were **ill-equipped** for such a sudden change in the weather.
8. Having fooled the townsfolk, the goblin gloated over his **ill-gotten** gains.
9. With his wily ways and **ill-favored** looks, the king's new advisor has few allies.
10. As the battle progressed, the general's **ill-conceived** plan soon unraveled.
11. "Ignore these **ill-boding** signs at your peril," cautioned the elfin queen.
12. "I can't stand an **ill-bred** child," sniffed Lady Bracknell.
13. The team looked on in despair at the **ill-faring** efforts of their captain.
14. "Being so **ill-mannered** is not going to get you very far," Hassan warned Amira.
15. "You would be **ill-advised** to challenge me," warned the witch.
16. Romeo and Juliet are famous for being **ill-fated** lovers.
17. Nobody could have foreseen that the venture would be so **ill-starred**.
18. "Why is everyone so **ill-disposed** towards my ideas?" whined Jeremy.
19. The king's decision to invade the neighboring country was **ill-judged**.
20. I didn't have the heart to tell Penny that her beloved puppy was rather **ill-looking**.

Spelling Test #14

1. A **hypocrite** is a person whose actions do not match their words.
2. An **agrarian** society is one whose economy is focused primarily on agriculture.
3. The woman denied she had any **affiliation** to the criminal gang.
4. The Chesapeake Bay is the largest **estuary** in the United States.
5. Once built, this factory will be dedicated to the **fabrication** of smart phones.
6. The adjective '**bovine**' can be used to describe something as 'relating to cattle'.
7. "Disobedience will result in **dire** consequences," the wizard warned.
8. The possible **longevity** of a red sea urchin is remarkable: two hundred years!
9. My brother has recently developed an interest in **calligraphy**.
10. The charlatan claimed that his potion was a **panacea** for all illnesses.
11. Kids will often **emulate** their parents' behavior.
12. The journalist had to sign a **confidentiality** agreement before doing the interview.
13. "Eureka!" yelled Byron. "I've just had an **epiphany**!"
14. The term '**schizophrenia**' was first used in the early years of the twentieth century.
15. **Acupuncture** is one of many treatments that derive from ancient Chinese medicine.
16. "This is an interesting **hypothesis**," said the physicist, "but it will need to be tested."
17. A '**sycophant**' is, in colloquial terms, someone who sucks up to another person.
18. After the mayor's unexpected announcement, the meeting descended into **anarchy**.
19. Astronomers are completely baffled by this strange **phenomenon**.
20. Nitric acid is formed from the **synthesis** of ammonia and oxygen.

Spelling Test #15

1. The architectural **achievements** of the ancient Romans are well-documented.
2. Reading regularly is one way to improve your **communication** skills.
3. Kindly fill out this **questionnaire** after the webinar has ended.
4. Becky was a **diligent** student; she always submitted her coursework on time.
5. Despite being fluent in French, Simona **occasionally** lapses into her native Romanian.
6. "Contact my press **liaison** officer if you have further queries," instructed the CEO.
7. Happy beyond words, Vanessa was certain she'd never felt so **buoyant**.
8. There is no rush to answer this email; you may reply at your **convenience**.
9. Aladdin's **perseverance** was finally rewarded when he discovered the vizier's hidden treasure.
10. Rick's **absence** was commented on by lots of people.
11. All over the world, the **occurrence** of extreme weather events is increasing.
12. Dr. Jones is regularly consulted for his archaeological **expertise**.
13. We **sincerely** regret that we cannot currently assist you in this matter.
14. Part of good oral **hygiene** is brushing your teeth regularly.
15. Tony raced down the street, **desperate** to make it to the station on time.
16. The valiant soldier was given a medal in **acknowledgment** of his outstanding bravery.
17. Carlos has not always been so **detached**; he used to be very sociable.
18. The **consensus** among my family is that my cousin doesn't exercise enough.
19. "This remarkable **opportunity** has allowed us to study this species," stated the botanist.
20. One of my favorite **accompaniments** to cheese is chutney.

Spelling Test #16

1. The crew of the *Black Skull* suffered an **ignominious** defeat at the hands of the French navy.
2. A reward of fifty gold **doubloons** was offered for Captain Jack's capture.
3. Many pirates died **inglorious** deaths.
4. Once found guilty of piracy, some people ended their lives on a **gibbet**.
5. One by one, the passengers made their way down the ship's **gangplank**.
6. To the Spanish, Sir Francis Drake was a **notorious** pirate.
7. **Marauding** pirates plagued the waters of the Mediterranean Sea for many years.
8. Barbary **corsairs** feature in a number of famous novels, including *Robinson Crusoe*.
9. Sir Henry Morgan made a fortune from **raiding** the Spanish Main.
10. The pirates were a band of cruel **cutthroats** who showed their victims no mercy.
11. Calico Jack was a pirate who was **infamous** for having two female crew members.
12. The pirates' **nefarious** plan included kidnapping the admiral's son.
13. "Aargh! I've dropped my **musket**!" yelled the pirate.
14. One government's **privateer** was another government's pirate.
15. "Alright, lads!" cried the **boatswain**. "It's time to get to work."
16. Grinning evilly, the pirate slowly removed his sharp **cutlass** from its scabbard.
17. After weeks of being lost, the crew decided they had no choice but to **mutiny**.
18. The first mate was furious when he learned of the captain's **double-dealing**.
19. "We are tormented by **buccaneers** who attack our treasure ships," complained the merchant.
20. The captain of the **galleon** had no idea that the pirates were already aboard.

Spelling Test #17

1	Having established there was no more food to be found, the duck **waddled** off.
2	After years of **roving** the globe, the world-famous naturalist decided to retire.
3	"Might I **escort** you to your table?" the waiter asked politely.
4	Having lost control of her bike, Wilma **careered** helplessly down the hill.
5	"Come on, kids," said Melissa as she **herded** the twins out of the candy store.
6	"I have **traversed** the world," said the hero, "and I have never seen a unicorn."
7	Farida **pranced** into the living room and declared she was going out.
8	Once class ended, the students **trooped** out into the corridor.
9	Unhappy with my decision, Leanne **flounced** off in a huff.
10	All Harry could do once his lie was discovered was **slink** away.
11	With nothing to do, Julian spent the afternoon **meandering** around his local mall.
12	"I think I'll **mosey** on down to the bookstore," Nigel announced.
13	When the fire alarm went off, all the employees **scrambled** to evacuate the building.
14	Carlos made his grandparents laugh as he **shepherded** them into the dining room.
15	"Knock before you enter; don't just **barge** in!" Tia scolded her younger brother.
16	"I can't walk in these high heels; the best I can do is **totter**," grumbled Maya.
17	"You don't have to **chaperone** me," said Ida crossly. "I can see myself out."
18	"No **loitering** outside the store," read the sign.
19	All I seem to do is **traipse** from one government office to the next.
20	We were **ushered** to our seats by an anxious-looking young man.

Spelling Test #18

1	Marsha nodded her head in **approval** at her sister's choice of pantsuit.
2	This novel offers a striking **portrayal** of life in contemporary Jamaica.
3	I found an excellent online **tutorial** on how to bake bread successfully.
4	The **acquittal** of the man accused of fraud surprised us all.
5	After all the awful things that had happened, they deserved a **reversal** of fortune.
6	"The **withdrawal** of our troops from the region is a priority," said the general.
7	Ravi frowned in **disapproval** at his naughty son.
8	Jeff's **proposal** that we swim in the freezing lake was met with silence.
9	"The species' **survival** is in the balance," warned the documentary maker.
10	"If we don't hurry, we're going to be late for our dress **rehearsal**," Selma warned.
11	The impoverished Lady Montague wanted an **appraisal** of her jewelry.
12	There is a strong, **confessional** streak to this celebrity's autobiography.
13	Last week, my mother attended a magnificent piano **recital**.
14	"I think my **dismissal** is completely unfair," fumed the angry employee.
15	The correct **disposal** of waste is something we should all take seriously.
16	The **dispersal** of the large, angry crowd took several hours.
17	Maria has a particular distaste for the **upheaval** that goes with redecorating.
18	The **deferral** of the exams has caused all sorts of complications.
19	Our **reappraisal** of the matter hasn't changed our views.
20	The Renaissance saw the **revival** of interest in ancient Greek and Roman literature.

Spelling Test #19

1. In the UK, **decorations** are awarded as part of the British 'honors system'.
2. "I would love to have an honorary degree **conferred** on me," said Harris wistfully.
3. Janice's approval was the highest **accolade** I could have asked for.
4. Most countries have special awards that they **bestow** on their outstanding citizens.
5. The king rewarded his loyal subject by giving him a **grant** of land.
6. We have been **commended** for setting up a local support group for the elderly.
7. "I refuse to pay **homage** to the usurper," said the rightful heir.
8. The director's last movie was very popular and received much critical **acclaim**.
9. Everything Joel does is designed to win the **approbation** of his peers.
10. On their return, the soldiers were **hailed** as heroes by their people.
11. "In **honor** of your victory, we shall have a banquet," King Arthur told Sir Lancelot.
12. As the general walked by, all his men **saluted** him.
13. My grandfather owned a large collection of **medals**.
14. The victorious team lifted the **trophy** amidst much celebration.
15. Ivy was amazed to learn that one of her ancestors was a politician of some **distinction**.
16. "**Tributes** to this famous musician are pouring in," announced the newsreader.
17. That blue **plaque** commemorates the birthplace of Charles Dickens.
18. Ten firefighters will be **decorated** for preventing the historic library from burning down.
19. The audience's **applause** at the end of the performance was deafening.
20. **Laurel** wreaths were awarded to the victors of the ancient Olympic Games.

Spelling Test #20

1. It can be difficult to **formulate** a simple sentence to express a complex idea.
2. Before email, people used to **correspond** by writing letters to each other.
3. In the Tower of London, you can see where prisoners **scratched** their names on the walls.
4. The ability to **communicate** effectively in writing is an important skill to have.
5. "I'm finding it hard to **verbalize** how I feel," admitted Sean.
6. Seeing the time, Olaf hastily **scribbled** a note to his wife before he rushed out.
7. Whenever my aunt sees my handwriting, she lectures me about my **penmanship**.
8. Having spent over ten hours **typing**, Ben developed cramp in his right hand.
9. 'Dear Sir or Madam' used to be a common **salutation** in formal writing.
10. That edition of the novel has space for students to **annotate** the text.
11. "Please, try to keep your answers **succinct**," the attorney requested.
12. Mabel's **signature** is completely illegible; I don't know how anyone can read it.
13. "Make sure to write your answers within the **margins**," instructed the teacher.
14. "You call those **squiggles** handwriting?" scoffed Martina.
15. When I was at school, my teachers insisted I learn **cursive** writing.
16. Polly decided that she needed to **rewrite** her composition before handing it in.
17. Working in **longhand** is easier than typing, I find.
18. While much fiction is full of beautiful descriptions, some can be rather **verbose**.
19. The detectives spent hours trying to decipher the **scrawl** at the bottom of the note.
20. This copy of the anthology is full of the poet's own **marginalia**.

Spelling Test #21

1. I **envision** that this process will take us three weeks to complete.
2. Ava found herself **entangled** in a bitter argument between her two best friends.
3. Days of fever had left Mr. Smythe wan and **enfeebled**.
4. The final section of the *Kryptos* sculpture remains **encoded**.
5. "Being rude will not **endear** you to anyone," Juan advised Paolo.
6. They walked along the beach in silence, their fingers **entwined**.
7. This festival promises to **encompass** a wide range of cultural activities and interests.
8. Despite many theories, we still do not know where Alexander the Great is **entombed**.
9. Overnight, the town was **engulfed** by a massive snowstorm.
10. Tiny diamonds **encircled** the ring's central sapphire.
11. We were completely **enthralled** by the sculptures we saw at the exhibition.
12. Suddenly, Lavinia realized she was **enmeshed** in a plot against the emperor.
13. "These changes shall be **enshrined** in law," the politician promised.
14. Vivian's opinion is firmly **entrenched**; there's no way you'll change her mind.
15. Many pieces of software claim to securely **encrypt** your messages, but do they really?
16. "'Blah' pretty much **encapsulates** how I feel at the moment," Rita said.
17. King Shahryar was **enraptured** by Scheherazade's nightly tales of adventure and mystery.
18. The more it struggled, the more the fly became **ensnared** in the spider's web.
19. "I think painting my room bright pink will **enliven** it," Nicky said.
20. After the Romans finally defeated the Gauls, many of them were **enslaved**.

Spelling Test #22

1. As he stepped out, Toby had to close his eyes against the **blinding** sunlight.
2. The queen's heavy, velvet cloak was shot through with **luminous** gold thread.
3. The **flickering** candle cast eerie shadows on the wall.
4. "**Blazing** fires have swept through these forests for days," the news anchor stated.
5. Riding across the plain, the knight's **burnished** armor made him an easy target.
6. There it lay, **glistening** on the beach: the largest conch that Simon had ever seen.
7. Kyle blinked against the car's **glaring** headlights.
8. Harris stopped as he noticed something **winking** in the undergrowth.
9. The **sparkling** eyes of the sorceress were an unusual shade of violet.
10. In the moonlight, the **shimmering** surface of the lake looked almost unreal.
11. Everywhere Aladdin turned, there were piles upon piles of **shining** treasure.
12. Outside in the courtyard, the pale moonlight **dappled** the large flagstones.
13. The temple was **ablaze** with the light of a thousand candles.
14. Penelope's attention was drawn to the faint, **glimmering** lights in the distance.
15. Crackling and **flaring**, the bonfire started to grow.
16. Cora screamed when she saw the wolf's **glittering** eyes.
17. Aida's new watch is all purple apart from the hands which are a **luminescent** green.
18. Mother-of-pearl has a distinctive **lustrous** quality.
19. When they were first built, the pyramids at Giza must have been **dazzling** to behold.
20. The peacock's tail is a **radiant** explosion of blues, greens, and purples.

Spelling Test #23

1. One of the uses of **chromium** is in the manufacture of stainless steel.
2. **Titanium** is biocompatible: it is nontoxic and is not rejected by the body.
3. Owing to its scarcity in the earth's crust, **platinum** is extremely valuable.
4. The filament in this bulb is made of **tungsten**.
5. Around thirteen million tonnes of **zinc** are produced every year.
6. 'Baking soda' is the common name for '**sodium** bicarbonate'.
7. An important component of nuclear weapons is **plutonium**.
8. Quinoa, spinach, and almonds are all sources of **magnesium**.
9. We're having **aluminum** window frames installed in the office.
10. An alternative name for **mercury** is 'quicksilver'.
11. "I suggest you clean that **brass** dish before you polish it," advised Farida.
12. Although it is a metal, **silver** is very soft.
13. Since it conducts both heat and electricity, **copper** has a wide range of uses.
14. I had no idea that **potassium** is used to make soap.
15. **Electrum** is a naturally-occurring alloy that was used by several ancient civilizations.
16. Did you know Rodin's **bronze** sculpture *The Thinker* was initially called *The Poet*?
17. **Nickel** is notable for its resistance to oxidation.
18. Both the ancient Romans and Egyptians used **pewter** to make decorative items.
19. **Uranium** is used in nuclear power stations to generate electricity.
20. A key component in the production of lithium-ion batteries is **cobalt**.

Spelling Test #24

1. Feeling **well-disposed** towards her brother, Alicia lent him her skateboard.
2. Although **well-meaning**, Tom's words only aggravated the situation.
3. Being **well-connected**, Julia knows many influential people in her industry.
4. "I know your efforts are **well-intentioned**, but I need to do this myself," said Justin.
5. Heads turned as the **well-groomed** couple entered the ballroom.
6. "Every other male character in that novel is described as '**well-favored**'," grumbled Pierre.
7. Since restructuring last year, the company has run like a **well-oiled** machine.
8. The scout was impressed by the high number of **well-conditioned** players on the field.
9. With its **well-appointed** suites and rooms, our local hotel has become a tourist magnet.
10. "You've got to be ridiculously **well-heeled** to shop at that boutique!" exclaimed Fred.
11. I was not happy to discover my suspicions had been **well-founded**.
12. "Your **well-affected** supporters will be key in this race," noted the campaign manager.
13. I think our team is **well-placed** to win this year's tournament.
14. "We aim to help young people grow into **well-rounded** individuals," declared the principal.
15. The eccentric billionaire left the entirety of his estate to his **well-beloved** dog.
16. Coach Martin is **well-liked** by his students and fellow faculty members.
17. Lady Bracknell's **well-ordered** household was the envy of her friends and acquaintances.
18. After a hectic year, Bernie treated himself to a **well-earned** break in Miami.
19. "You would be **well-advised** to address these issues now," Fran's accountant urged her.
20. Being **well-grounded** in research methodologies has been invaluable to me.

Spelling Test #25

1. Aki was **agreeably** surprised when she saw how much was in her checking account.
2. Dervla has always had a tendency to behave **unpredictably**.
3. My neighbor is great, but he does have a habit of talking **incessantly**.
4. **Paradoxically**, his life was saved because he was ill.
5. While his sister wasn't looking, Oscar **covertly** hid her birthday present in his closet.
6. I spent ten minutes **feverishly** hunting in my purse for the house keys.
7. The dignitaries **sedately** took their places around the table.
8. As the music got faster, the dancers moved ever more **frenetically**.
9. The moment the bell rang, Gloria sprang **lithely** to her feet.
10. Luna **haphazardly** tipped the contents of the tote bag onto her bed.
11. "I'm afraid I can't answer that," replied Jed **elusively**.
12. We have been working **diligently** all week to get our assignments finished.
13. The twins were **staunchly** opposed to Amani's suggestion.
14. "There's no need for you to be mean to me," said Quentin **reproachfully**.
15. "Have you considered the fact that he might be right?" she asked **tactfully**.
16. Under certain conditions, hay can **spontaneously** combust.
17. Lucas has **begrudgingly** accepted that he needs to apologize to Marcia.
18. **Lamentably**, we are unable to help you at this time.
19. "Well, if you don't know, why should I?" Eric asked **obnoxiously**.
20. "I **fervently** wish that this had never happened," said Zenobia sincerely.

Spelling Test #26

1. He noticed that droplets of water had **condensed** on the windowpane.
2. We stared in horror as the water **gushed** out of the widening cracks in the dam.
3. Owing to the amount of recent rain, the ground is completely **saturated**.
4. The flowers had died because all the water in their vase had **evaporated**.
5. Sheila noticed a thin **trickle** of blood just below her left knee.
6. "Ugh! I hate it when it **drizzles**!" complained Betty.
7. Make sure that you completely **immerse** the fabric in the dye.
8. If the rain doesn't stop soon, rivers are going to start **overflowing**.
9. "Did you remember to **flush**?" the young boy's mother asked him.
10. The noise the water made as it **cascaded** over the rocks was deafening.
11. "I'd **soak** that shirt before putting it in the washing machine," advised Cleo.
12. "It is crucial that these fields are **irrigated** properly," the farmer told us.
13. Once the river burst its banks, it took just an hour for the entire village to be **swamped**.
14. At around ten o'clock in the morning, lava began to **spurt** out of the volcano.
15. Tarek wiped a **dribble** of milk from the corner of his baby son's mouth.
16. When they arrived, the engineers could clearly see the well was still **spouting** oil.
17. **Precipitation** is measured using a rain gauge.
18. Last week, I got **drenched** in a thunderstorm that came out of nowhere.
19. This **submerged** shipwreck has been a magnet for treasure hunters for years.
20. For centuries in Egypt, the **inundation** of the Nile was an annual event.

Spelling Test #27

1. Kimberly's feeling of **déjà vu** unsettled her; she knew she'd not been there before.
2. "The **double entendre** in the song's title is fun — even if it is a bit naughty," confessed Gina.
3. After our turbulent flight, we were relieved to be back on **terra firma**.
4. He's given me **carte blanche** to make any changes to the design I want.
5. "**Mea culpa**!" cried the fairy. "This is all my fault! Please, forgive me!"
6. "Can you see anything?" whispered Alan **sotto voce**.
7. "Certain dangerous ideas MUST be contained by a **cordon sanitaire**," argued the activist.
8. During the Renaissance, a person might keep a human skull as a **memento mori**.
9. "We must remain **in situ** as we carry out our security check," said the flight attendant.
10. Ricky loves French **haute cuisine**; I prefer less complicated food.
11. '**Enfant terrible**' can refer to a young person who adopts an unorthodox approach to things.
12. They are renovating that building to preserve its **beaux arts** features.
13. Since my parents are away, my Uncle Jove is acting **in loco parentis**.
14. Nick prefers his spaghetti **al dente**: with a bit of bite to it.
15. The statement is not wrong **per se**, but it is vague.
16. Being a night owl, Iris is never **compos mentis** before 10 o'clock.
17. As Sir Thomas Overbury had fled to France, the English court tried him **in absentia**.
18. "Do whatever you want!" said Harry with an airy **laissez-faire** attitude.
19. Given her terrible behavior at my last party, Beatrice is now **persona non grata**.
20. "I'm afraid it's a **fait accompli**; nothing can be changed now," apologized Fran.

Spelling Test #28

1. The small ship rocked gently on the waves as it lay **anchored** outside the port.
2. Sylvia is a complete **technology** buff; it's all she can talk about.
3. Patty came up with a crazy **scheme** to discover who stole her bicycle.
4. During the nineteenth century, **cholera** swept across the globe.
5. The **chimera** is a mythical monster with a lion's head, a goat's body, and a serpent's tail.
6. Dean spent hours digging through the local **archives** in search of a clue.
7. **Orchids** are my least favorite flowers.
8. Many scientists — including Sir Isaac Newton — have been intrigued by **alchemy**.
9. In humans, the **trachea** is found immediately in front of the esophagus.
10. The earliest known usage of the word '**chemotherapy**' is 1910.
11. "Of course, we didn't tell her!" came the **chorus** of denials from his friends.
12. The human **psyche** has long been a subject of serious study.
13. Artists' use of red **ocher** stretches back to prehistoric times.
14. "With such a beautiful voice, have you considered becoming a **chorister**?" Ida asked.
15. Within the **hierarchy** of the British aristocracy, a duke ranks the highest.
16. Many **scholarly** books have been written about Shakespeare's life.
17. "I love the opening **chords** of that song!" enthused Wendy.
18. '**Archaic**' is used to describe words that used to be common, but which are now rare.
19. Reaching the end of the tunnel, the explorer found a great **chasm** before him.
20. Poor Amelia suffers from **chronic** indigestion; she always has a stomachache.

Spelling Test #29

1. Rania spent the whole afternoon watching game **demos**.
2. The **game pad** has replaced things like joysticks, paddles, and keypads.
3. "You can get additional **downloadable** costumes for your character," Kim told Sally.
4. "I've completed over a hundred **quests** in that game," Lucy announced proudly.
5. "I've tried the **single-player** option in that game, but I think it's boring," commented Yara.
6. "Have you used this **cheat code**? It unlocks a secret level!" said Chen excitedly.
7. That game is available on all the major **platforms**.
8. Shona was unimpressed by the game's **graphics**; they looked dated.
9. "This game's **interface** is confusing; I can't see how to do anything," complained Greg.
10. "Which **avatar** did you select?" Jamila asked Omar. "I chose the goblin king."
11. This racing game has been updated to support **multiplayer** mode.
12. My brothers have always been really good at **shoot-'em-ups**; I'm terrible at them.
13. When I first tried a **virtual reality** headset, I became a bit nauseous.
14. This new **role-playing game** offers highly immersive fantasy worlds for players to explore.
15. "I prefer **split screen** games so that I can compete against my friends," said Ed.
16. Michel's parents promised to buy him a new game **console** for his birthday.
17. "Something is wrong with the **controller**; the buttons keep sticking," observed Ravi.
18. A hundred years ago, **artificial intelligence** was pure science fiction.
19. **Handheld** devices have revolutionized our lives in innumerable ways.
20. There's a bug in the **game engine**; you can't get beyond level thirty.

Spelling Test #30

1. My grandmother gave me an **exquisite** Victorian brooch for my eighteenth birthday.
2. When a currency is **debased**, this means its value is lowered.
3. Mrs. Fischer ran a highly **profitable** business selling personalized coffee mugs.
4. "Please, be careful with that statuette!" begged Tina. "It is **irreplaceable**!"
5. "A million dollars is no **trifling** sum," Michaela observed.
6. "I'm not getting into this **petty** debate; I've got better things to do," said Pat.
7. "I'm afraid that this painting is a fake; it is **valueless**," the auctioneer told me.
8. His **laudable** efforts to help his local community were recognized by the mayor.
9. I think this election will be **inconsequential**; I don't believe it will change anything.
10. Insultingly, the merchant offered the lad a **paltry** sum as a reward.
11. His grandfather's diary is one of his most **treasured** possessions.
12. The governor should be dealing with the big issues, not **trivial** matters.
13. "It gives me great pleasure to introduce our **esteemed** guest," announced Mr. Franklin.
14. I have always **cherished** the small medallion that my uncle gave me.
15. The worth of this manuscript is **inestimable**; it is one of a kind.
16. That day, the young shepherd learned a **valuable** lesson in humility.
17. "What a lazy, **good-for-nothing** boy you are!" Tom's aunt scolded.
18. His behavior at the meeting was utterly **contemptible**.
19. Cheap jewelry doesn't have to be **tawdry**; there are ways to make it look good.
20. "Your efforts have made a **substantial** contribution to the company," my boss said.

Spelling Test #31

1. The poor horses found themselves **laden** with heavy saddlebags.
2. Vitamin D is meant to help **strengthen** bones and teeth.
3. We need to find a way to **lessen** the negative impact of this.
4. The king's counselors **hastened** to inform him of the dragons' arrival.
5. "If you need to **unburden** yourself, you can always talk to me," Lyra told Alice supportively.
6. Chris was utterly **maddened** by Ro's selfish behavior.
7. Billy was **chastened** when he realized he had misjudged his brother.
8. Olivia loves her curly hair, so she never tries to **straighten** it.
9. "Come on! Don't be **disheartened**! It's not over yet!" Harriet urged.
10. We are always looking for ways to **heighten** students' enjoyment of learning.
11. "Can I have something to help **deaden** the pain?" Brian asked his dentist.
12. According to legend, King Arthur will **reawaken** when Britain needs him again.
13. The makers of this hand cream claim it **smoothens** your skin in a week.
14. "I didn't tell you this before as I didn't want to **overburden** you," Marina explained.
15. The suspect **moistened** his lips nervously before answering the question.
16. "**Hearken** to my advice, or calamity will befall the kingdom," the old crone cautioned.
17. The fairy's smile **emboldened** the shepherd to approach her.
18. "Can you **unfasten** these cuff links for me?" Mr. Romano asked his wife.
19. Doing a lot of manual work is likely to **coarsen** your hands.
20. "Now is not the time to **slacken**! We must keep forging ahead!" cried the general.

Spelling Test #32

1. Although the images were **gruesome**, we could not tear our eyes away from them.
2. For the Elizabethans, regicide was a most **heinous** crime.
3. "Your **repugnant** actions leave me with no choice," the judge told the defendant sternly.
4. The family were devastated by the **distressing** news.
5. "I can't abide Mr. Collins," said Lydia. "I've never met a more **odious** man."
6. "I love my sister dearly, but her taste in clothes is **horrendous**," confessed Janice.
7. "I always enjoy a story with a **detestable** villain," declared Armand.
8. The duke's betrayal of his younger brother was utterly **despicable**.
9. Excessive competitiveness in an office can lead to an **unwholesome** workplace.
10. It is not yet known how many people were injured in the **appalling** accident.
11. The king's chief advisor was a **loathsome** man; he had no scruples to speak of.
12. "I find any kind of deceit **abhorrent**," said Rosa primly.
13. As the samurai warriors entered the temple, a **ghastly** sight met their eyes.
14. The **abominable** crimes committed by the gang have shocked the whole state.
15. That magazine always prints **objectionable** photos of celebrities.
16. "The weather has been **atrocious** recently; it's rained constantly," Ivy told me.
17. The smell of the rotten food was **nauseating**.
18. Mixing certain chemical substances can produce **noxious** fumes.
19. "Yes," Gillian agreed. "Marcus's joke was **distasteful**."
20. "I can't eat with him; his table manners are so **gross**!" exclaimed Daisy.

Spelling Test #33

1	"These letters provide interesting insights into the **rebellion**," noted the historian.
2	Some people think Shakespeare's history plays are best read in **chronological** order.
3	In geology, an '**epoch**' is a unit of time greater than an 'age', but less than a 'period'.
4	In 1381, the English **peasantry** revolted against the imposition of new taxes.
5	After the assassination of Julius Caesar, the Romans descended into **civil war**.
6	The first work by Plato that I read was *The **Republic***.
7	Renaissance paintings are a **testament** to the cultural impact of ancient Greek myths.
8	The worship of multiple gods and goddesses was common in **antiquity**.
9	The removal of the **monarchy** enabled the army to seize control of the country.
10	"The proposed changes to their **constitution** are sure to ignite debate," observed Ada.
11	"The available **documentation** does not support your claim," argued the scholar.
12	At the time of his death, the tribe's **patriarch** had ruled for forty years.
13	*The **Annals*** is a work by Tacitus that charts the history of the Roman Empire.
14	"We must do everything we can to preserve our **democracy**!" declared the politician.
15	In many countries, the **legislature** is called the National Assembly.
16	During the French Revolution, members of the **aristocracy** were executed on the guillotine.
17	Our local museum boasts an impressive collection of **prehistoric** tools.
18	'**Bourgeoisie**' can be used to mean 'middle class'.
19	Queen Elizabeth II is currently the UK's longest-reigning **sovereign**.
20	Over the centuries, many philosophers have written treatises on the subject of **tyranny**.

Spelling Test #34

1	Try as he might, Rick could not **outpace** his sister.
2	"What unites these companies is the fact that they are **outliers**," said the economist.
3	The school had to be closed following an **outbreak** of chicken pox.
4	In exams, Nat has always **outperformed** most of his peers.
5	My cousin Edna has just started working at an **outreach** center for the homeless.
6	When the attack came from behind, the soldiers realized they'd been **outflanked**.
7	There was an **outpouring** of support for the victims of the earthquake.
8	Some of this work will have to be **outsourced**; there's too much here for us to do.
9	"I'm always worried that I will **outstay** my welcome," admitted Marianne.
10	This year's election is very close; it is impossible to predict the **outcome**.
11	The little boy ran to his mother's **outstretched** arms.
12	In our class, the girls **outnumber** the boys by two to one.
13	Under the circumstances, Ivan's angry **outburst** was entirely predictable.
14	Last year, the factory's **output** dropped by roughly twenty percent.
15	I never play chess with Brad; he always completely **outmaneuvers** me.
16	Odysseus came up with a cunning plan to **outwit** the Trojans.
17	"Your legacy, sire, will **outlast** us all," the vizier promised the sultan.
18	The sheriff and his men found themselves **outgunned** by the outlaws.
19	"I think the benefits of this plan **outweigh** its risks," agreed Cecile.
20	"The well that you seek lies on the **outskirts** of the village of Arden," said the witch.

Spelling Test #35

1. "That **trailer** is terrible; it's full of spoilers!" complained Wendy.
2. The use of **computer-generated** imagery is now a staple of filmmaking.
3. The **scriptwriter** argued long and hard over the changes the producers wanted to make.
4. The studio is set to announce the date for the **premiere** of its latest blockbuster.
5. "I saw several **clips** from that movie on TV," Lionel said.
6. "I can't name my favorite **animated** cartoon; there are too many!" laughed Carlos.
7. "I found this movie's use of actual war **footage** very moving," said the critic.
8. Some members of the **audience** complained that the sound was too loud.
9. It is now odd to think that, in theaters, movies were once shown with an **intermission**.
10. Apparently, a new **biopic** about Elvis Presley has gone into production.
11. Her office walls were covered with **freeze-frames** from the movies she'd worked on.
12. Their latest **documentary** has been nominated for several awards.
13. Disappointingly, the **release** of the movie has been delayed again.
14. In the future, we want **audio description** for customers to be the norm, not the exception.
15. Can you name five influential **choreographers** of the twentieth century?
16. Every film studio dreams of coming up with the next big **franchise**.
17. As the movie reached its terrifying climax, the **auditorium** was completely silent.
18. "Is this Italian movie available with English **subtitles**?" the customer asked.
19. That director's movies are always filmed on **location** in Canada.
20. Deservedly, the movie won the Oscar for Best Original **Screenplay**.

Spelling Test #36

1. "The **toxicity** level of the soil is regularly checked," said the scientist.
2. Vera's cheerfulness and **vivacity** made her extremely popular at work.
3. The spy's **duplicity** resulted in many state secrets being shared with the enemy.
4. People are outraged by this **atrocity**.
5. The **ferocity** of Linus's denial took Paulina by surprise.
6. "Given the **paucity** of evidence, it is impossible to arrive at a conclusion," Jo noted.
7. Police officers have arrested a man for suspected **complicity** in the heist.
8. It took Angelica hours to check the **veracity** of the information in her article.
9. The ballet dancers gave a performance that was perfect in its **synchronicity**.
10. Sadly, some of Pete's neighbors were not very tolerant of his **eccentricity**.
11. The opposite of 'transparency' is '**opacity**'.
12. I find her **incapacity** to take responsibility for her mistakes infuriating.
13. The **authenticity** of the painting has been questioned by an art historian.
14. The increasing **scarcity** of many species is a cause for genuine concern.
15. "I can't believe Bob had the **audacity** to take my phone without asking!" fumed Otto.
16. The king's growing **egocentricity** began to make him unpopular with his people.
17. Many advertisements use scenes of comfortable **domesticity** to promote products.
18. "The **tenacity** of this stain is really annoying; it won't come out," grumbled Mark.
19. The narrative is very rich and is thus open to a **multiplicity** of interpretations.
20. One example of '**reciprocity**' is when two people help each other.

Spelling Test #37

1. No longer used, the **encyclopedia** sat on the top shelf gathering dust.
2. Further illustrative tables can be found in the book's **appendix**.
3. That book needs a **glossary**; it's full of words I've never seen before.
4. One possible use of a **prologue** is to pique the audience's curiosity.
5. "The **dedication** to the author's father is incredibly moving," said Eve.
6. '**Plagiarism**' is stealing someone else's work and pretending that it's yours.
7. As Indira loves words, she spends hours reading entries in her **thesaurus**.
8. I've just discovered *Bored of the Rings*: a **parody** of Tolkien's *Lord of the Rings* trilogy.
9. The **pagination** in this document is incorrect; it jumps from page five to page ten.
10. You are far more likely to find **footnotes** in a scholarly work than in a novel.
11. Unusually, the story is told from the **perspective** of the hero's horse.
12. **Allegories** are often used by writers as a way of talking about controversial ideas.
13. The autobiography began with an **anecdote** from the writer's childhood.
14. To write an effective **satire**, you need to understand the work you are criticizing.
15. A book's **preface** is to be found at its beginning.
16. The death of a dog **foreshadows** the death of the main character later on.
17. It's impossible to find anything in that book; it doesn't have an **index**.
18. "That novel's **epigraph** didn't work; it didn't relate to the story at all," Keira said.
19. '**Protagonist**' is a single word that means 'main character'.
20. "Why are you reading the book's **epilogue** first?" Max asked in amazement.

Spelling Test #38

1. As the performers took their places, the kids gazed on in rapt **fascination**.
2. "Look! That poster says the **juggler** performs blindfolded!" Rick said excitedly.
3. Bouncing up and down on the **trampoline**, the clowns kept trying to push one another off.
4. **Hippodromes** were originally ancient Greek stadiums used for horse and chariot races.
5. I've always wanted to try walking on **stilts**, but I'm scared of heights.
6. With **death-defying** bravery, the young girl stepped onto the tightrope.
7. **Audaciously**, the clown crept up behind the magician and grabbed his hat.
8. Everyone gasped as the **contortionist** twisted into a seemingly impossible shape.
9. The spellbinding feats of the **aerialist** left her audience breathless.
10. The performers that the twins most enjoyed were the **somersaulting** clowns.
11. "It must take hours to sew all those **sequins** onto those costumes," observed Sula.
12. "The cost of **admission** for children under twelve is $5," read the sign.
13. "I can't watch!" squeaked Zeinab as the **snake charmer** draped a python round his neck.
14. When he went to the circus, Tommy was captivated by the **fire-eater**.
15. A **sword-swallower** is a performer who passes a long blade down their throat into their stomach.
16. As the **ringmaster** stepped out before the crowd, all the lights went off save one.
17. "The performance I most want to see is that of the **hula hooper**," confided Amy.
18. "I thought the **trapeze** artists were particularly mesmerizing," said Lucy.
19. The kids laughed at the antics of the **troupe** of mischievous monkeys.
20. We were enthralled by the stunning **acrobatic** feats taking place high above us.

Spelling Test #39

1. "Oh, **fiddlesticks**!" said Cordelia crossly. "I've burnt my toast again."
2. "I know you love your **jalopy**, but isn't it time you bought a new car?" Arvind asked.
3. "Don't call your brother an **ignoramus**!" scolded Vicki's mother.
4. Although it had seen better days, the mansion retained an air of **genteel** elegance.
5. As more people arrived, our lawn party turned into a fully-fledged **jamboree**.
6. In their **heyday**, that boy band sold more tickets than any other group.
7. Some dishonest caller **bamboozled** my grandpa into giving them fifty dollars.
8. Ursula is researching accounts of infamous nineteenth-century **desperadoes**.
9. We were all **agog**, waiting to see what would happen next.
10. My friend Sookie was in the **doldrums**, so I went round to try to cheer her up.
11. "I know the truth: I know that you and Jane are in **cahoots**," stated Freddy.
12. The mayor and his wife were greeted by loud **huzzahs** and clapping.
13. "That is completely untrue! Utter **balderdash**!" spluttered Brian.
14. It's impossible to get a sensible answer out of Julian; he spouts nothing but **hogwash**.
15. Played by Australian Aborigines, the **didgeridoo** is a long, wooden wind instrument.
16. "I've got an **ironclad** alibi," the suspect smugly told the detective.
17. The authorities warned the protesters that they would not be allowed to run **amok**.
18. The family lunch descended into **bedlam** when a fire started in the kitchen.
19. "I have no idea how to work this **gizmo**!" grumbled Jorge irritably.
20. In the old portrait stood a distinguished, middle-aged gentleman wearing a **fez**.

SUGGESTED ANSWERS:
VOCABULARY BUILDERS, SYNONYM SPOTTERS, & ANTONYM ALERTS

For your convenience, we have provided a selection of possible answers to the student prompts included in the relevant Vocabulary Builders, Synonym Spotters, & Antonym Alerts throughout this workbook.

Please note, however, that these answers are intended as guidelines only.
Your child may well come up with alternative, correct answers of their own.

#3 Sherlock Holmes & Co. (p. 9)
Vocabulary Builder:
Watching-related words: shadowing | surveillance

#4 They Asked, We Replied (p. 11)
Synonym Spotting:
beseeched = pleaded
responded = retorted
lectured = preached

#9 Sound Effects (p. 21)
Antonym Alert:
rhythmic ≠ irregular
tumultuous ≠ silent

Synonym Spotting:
raucous = tumultuous
resonant = sonorous
tumultuous = blaring

#10 The Age of Chivalry? (p. 23)
Vocabulary Builder:
Writing-related words: chronicles | parchment

#12 Spoiled for Choice I (p. 27)
Vocabulary Builder:
Adjectives to describe people: avaricious | feisty | intrepid

#13 Ill- The Ill-Informed (p. 29)
Synonym Spotter:
ill-advised = ill-judged
ill-fated = ill-starred
ill-favored = ill-looking

#14 Ancient Origins (p. 31)
Vocabulary Builder:
Dishonesty-related words: fabrication | hypocrite | sycophant

#16 Pirates!! (p. 35)
Synonym Spotting:
inglorious = shameful
marauding = pillaging
mutiny = rebellion = insurrection

#17 Left, Right, Left, Right... (p. 37)
Vocabulary Builder:
Additional verbs: accompany | conduct | guide | lurch | plod | stagger | trudge

#19 And the Winner is... (p. 41)
Synonym Spotting:
accolade = citation
homage = adulation
saluted = acknowledged

#20 Dotting I's & Crossing T's (p. 43)
Vocabulary Builder:
Words related to conveying meaning: communicate | correspond | verbalize

#21 En- The Enriched (p. 45)
Synonym Spotting:
encapsulates = summarizes
enfeebled = weakened
entrenched = lodged

#22 Light Effects (p. 47)
Antonym Alert:
lustrous ≠ dull OR lackluster

radiant ≠ dim
shining ≠ matte

Vocabulary Builder:
Candle-related words: blazing | flaring | flickering | winking

#23 All that Glitters... (p. 49)
Vocabulary Builder:
Greek & Roman mythology-related: mercury | plutonium | titanium | uranium

#24 Well- The Well-Fed (p. 51)
Vocabulary Builder:
Appearance-related words: well-favored | well-groomed

#25 Spoiled for Choice II (p. 53)
Synonym Spotting:
diligently = conscientiously
haphazardly = disorderly
sedately = solemnly

Antonym Alert:
agreeably ≠ disagreeably
covertly ≠ overtly
tactfully ≠ tactlessly

#26 Drip...Drip...Drip (p. 55)
Synonym Spotting:
immerse = submerse
irrigated = watered

Antonym Alert:
dribble ≠ stream
soak ≠ parch

#27 Loanwords (p. 57)
Vocabulary Builder:
Troublesome people: enfant terrible | persona non grata

#28 'Ch' is for 'Chaos' (p. 59)
Vocabulary Builder:
Music words: chords | chorister | chorus

#31 Happy Endings III (p. 65)
Antonym Alert:
hastened ≠ dawdled
strengthen ≠ weaken

unfasten ≠ fasten

#33 Bygone Days (p. 69)
Vocabulary Builder:
Rulers: patriarch | sovereign

#34 Out- The Outnumbered (p. 71)
Vocabulary Builder:
Words to describe emotions: outburst | outpouring

#35 The Silver Screen (p. 73)
Vocabulary Builder:
Extracts or parts of movies: clips | freeze-frames | trailer

#36 City Central (p. 75)
Synonym & Antonym Soup:
egocentricity = selfishness
scarcity = shortage
vivacity = liveliness

egocentricity ≠ selflessness
scarcity ≠ abundance
vivacity ≠ inactivity

Vocabulary Builder:
Violence-related words: atrocity | ferocity

#37 Bookish Business (p. 77)
Vocabulary Builder:
Reference books: encyclopedia | thesaurus

Antonym Alert:
footnotes ≠ endnotes
plagiarism ≠ origination
protagonist ≠ antagonist

#38 The Big Top (p. 79)
Vocabulary Builder:
Gymnastics-related words: acrobatic | somersaulting | trampoline | trapeze

#39 That's a Proper Word?!?! (p. 81)
Synonym Spotting:
amok = wildly
bedlam = chaos
doldrums = dejection
heyday = golden age

INDEX I

This index organizes the units in this workbook according to their target areas. The entries in each main category are listed in alphabetical order.

SPELLING PATTERNS

Commonly Mistaken Spellings: #15 That Doesn't Look Right... (p. 33)

Compound Words: Hyphenated Adjectives with ill-: #13 Ill- The Ill-Informed (p. 29)
Compound Words: Hyphenated Adjectives with well-: #24 Well- The Well-Fed (p. 51)

Doubled Consonants: #1 Double Trouble (p. 5)

Letter String 'ch' as 'k': #28 'Ch' is for 'Chaos' (p. 59)

Prefix en-: #21 En- The Enriched (p. 45)
Prefix out-: #34 Out- The Outnumbered (p. 71)
Prefix un-: #5 Un- The Unheeded (p. 13)

Suffix -age: #8 Happy Endings I (p. 19)
Suffix -al: #18 Happy Endings II (p. 39)
Suffix -en: #31 Happy Endings III (p. 65)
Suffix -ity: #36 City Central (p. 75)
Suffix -ness: #11 Nessing Things Up (p. 25)

Words from Other Languages: Greek & Latin: #14 Ancient Origins (p. 31)
Words from Other Languages: Loanwords: #27 Loanwords (p. 57)

THEMED AREAS OF GENERAL KNOWLEDGE

Awards: #19 And the Winner is... (p. 41)
Books: #37 Bookish Business (p. 77)
Cinema & Film: #35 The Silver Screen (p. 73)
Detectives: #3 Sherlock Holmes & Co. (p. 9)
Friendship & Enmity: #2 Friend...Or Foe? (p. 7)
Hunting & Hunters: #7 The Game is Afoot (p. 17)
Metals & Alloys: #23 All that Glitters... (p. 49)
Pirates: #16 Pirates!! (p. 35)
Political & Social History: #33 Bygone Days (p. 69)

The Circus: #38 The Big Top (p. 79)
The Middle Ages: #10 The Age of Chivalry? (p. 23)
Video Games: #29 Player 1 is Ready (p. 61)
Water: #26 Drip...Drip...Drip (p. 55)
Writing: #20 Dotting I's & Crossing T's (p. 43)

USEFUL ALTERNATIVE VOCABULARY

Antonym Pair: Valued vs Worthless: #30 What's it Worth? (p. 63)
'Awful' Synonyms: #32 How Awful! (p. 67)
'Said' Synonyms: #4 They Asked, We Replied (p. 11)
'Silly' Synonyms: #6 That's Just Plain Silly! (p. 15)
'Walk' Synonyms: #17 Left, Right, Left, Right... (p. 37)

WORDS FOR CREATIVE WRITING

Fun Words: #39 That's a Proper Word?!?! (p. 81)
Light: #22 Light Effects (p. 47)
Mixed Adjectives: #12 Spoiled for Choice I (p. 27)
Mixed Adverbs: #25 Spoiled for Choice II (p. 53)
Sounds: #9 Sound Effects (p. 21)

INDEX II

This index lists the units in order with a brief key to the area each unit targets.

....

UNITS

#1 Double Trouble (p. 5): Spelling Patterns: Doubled Consonants

#2 Friend...Or Foe? (p. 7): Themed: Friendship & Enmity

#3 Sherlock Holmes & Co. (p. 9): Themed: Detectives

#4 They Asked, We Replied (p. 11): Vocabulary: 'Said' Synonyms

#5 Un- The Unheeded (p. 13): Spelling Patterns: Prefix un-

#6 That's Just Plain Silly! (p. 15): Vocabulary: 'Silly' Synonyms

#7 The Game is Afoot (p. 17): Themed: Hunting & Hunters

#8 Happy Endings I (p. 19): Spelling Patterns: Suffix -age

#9 Sound Effects (p. 21): Creative Writing: Sounds

#10 The Age of Chivalry? (p. 23): Themed: The Middle Ages

#11 Nessing Things Up (p. 25): Spelling Patterns: Suffix -ness

#12 Spoiled for Choice I (p. 27): Creative Writing: Mixed Adjectives

#13 Ill- The Ill-Informed (p. 29): Spelling Patterns: Compound Words: Hyphenated Adjectives with ill-

#14 Ancient Origins (p. 31): Spelling Patterns: Words from Other Languages: Greek & Latin

#15 That Doesn't Look Right... (p. 33): Spelling Patterns: Commonly Mistaken Spellings

#16 Pirates!! (p. 35): Themed: Pirates

#17 Left, Right, Left, Right... (p. 37): Vocabulary: 'Walk' Synonyms

#18 Happy Endings II (p. 39): Spelling Patterns: Suffix -al

#19 And the Winner is... (p. 41): Themed: Awards

#20 Dotting I's & Crossing T's (p. 43): Themed: Writing

#21 En- The Enriched (p. 45): Spelling Patterns: Prefix en-

#22 Light Effects (p. 47): Creative Writing: Light

#23 All that Glitters... (p. 49): Themed: Metals & Alloys

#24 Well- The Well-Fed (p. 51): Spelling Patterns: Compound Words: Hyphenated Adjectives with well-

#25 Spoiled for Choice II (p. 53): Creative Writing: Mixed Adverbs

#26 Drip...Drip...Drip (p. 55): Themed: Water

#27 Loanwords (p. 57): Spelling Patterns: Words from Other Languages: Loanwords

#28 'Ch' is for 'Chaos' (p. 59): Spelling Patterns: Letter String 'ch' as 'k'

#29 Player 1 is Ready (p. 61): Themed: Video Games

#30 What's it Worth? (p. 63): Vocabulary: Antonym Pair: Valued vs Worthless

#31 Happy Endings III (p. 65): Spelling Patterns: Suffix -en

#32 How Awful! (p. 67): Vocabulary: 'Awful' Synonyms

#33 Bygone Days (p. 69): Themed: Political & Social History

#34 Out- The Outnumbered (p. 71): Spelling Patterns: Prefix out-

#35 The Silver Screen (p. 73): Themed: Cinema & Film

#36 City Central (p. 75): Spelling Patterns: Suffix -ity

....

BONUS UNITS

#37 Bookish Business (p. 77): Themed: Books

#38 The Big Top (p. 79): Themed: The Circus

#39 That's a Proper Word?!?! (p. 81): Creative Writing: Fun Words

Made in the USA
Las Vegas, NV
30 September 2023